LECTURES IN ECONOMICS 5

TOPICS IN APPLIED ECONOMETRICS

Kenneth F. Wallis

The London School of Economics and Political Science

GRAY—MILLS PUBLISHING LTD.
10 Juer Street
London, S.W.11

First edition 1973

ISBN 085641 011 x (paper)
ISBN 085641 010 1 (cloth)

Printed in Great Britain by
Lowe & Brydone (Printers) Ltd., Haverhill, Suffolk

CONTENTS

PREFACE

This book originated in a course of lectures given at the London School of Economics to students on the M.Sc. course in Economics in 1970-71, as a sequel to my *Introductory Econometrics* course, already published in this series. The lectures were tape-recorded and transcribed by Hamish Gray and Donna Hamway, and although a substantial amount of editing and revising has subsequently taken place, the result is more lecture notes than treatise.

The object of the course and of this book is to discuss the problems of formulating and empirically testing economic hypotheses by considering in some detail a few specific areas of application that are nevertheless of considerable general interest. These "case studies" follow the general introduction to the methods of econometrics mentioned above, and emphasise the interplay of economic theory and econometric techniques. The aim is not to present a survey of empirical work on each of the chosen topics, but simply to select a few instructive examples in each area to illustrate both the general principles and the local difficulties. When the conclusion is that considerable local difficulties remain to be tackled, hopefully some students will find it encouraging that there is still work to be done.

The basic topics are consumption, production, and investment functions, and macroeconometric models, as can be seen from the course reading list, reproduced in the Appendix. The main additions to the lecture course are the discussions of distributed lags, a demand and supply model, and the final form of dynamic models, the last of which comes from some later lectures on "Further Methods of Economic Investigation". The only deletion is the detailed consideration of a current macroeconometric model, for the particular specifications of operational models are continually changing, and our emphasis is on the general application of such models.

Although from time to time there are references to my *Introductory Econometrics* (abbreviated to *IE*), this book is self-contained, for the references are generally to discussions of basic technical points, and many alternative presentations of such material exist. While it is hoped that readers of other theoretical texts will find this discussion of applied problems useful, *IE* nonetheless provides the most accurate indication of what prior knowledge is assumed, and the terminology and notation are consistent. The opportunity has also been taken to refer to Stephen Glaister's *Mathematical Methods for Economists*, which provides a useful mathematical background, unfortunately not available when this course was first given.

I am grateful to David Hendry and Meghnad Desai whose comments and suggestions have been of great benefit, and to Carol Martin whose secretarial assistance has been invaluable. Errors of omission and commission are, as usual, my own responsibility.

Chapter 1

THE CONSUMPTION FUNCTION

Introduction

The consumption function was frequently used as a simple illustration in *Introductory Econometrics*, and its theoretical underpinnings are discussed in Professor Johnson's *Macroeconomics and Monetary Theory*. Here also it provides a useful first topic. We retrace the steps taken in developing and testing consumption theories, indicating the interactions between theory and empirical evidence, then discuss a study which in addition uses some theoretical statistical results about instrumental variable estimators to test a particular theory, and conclude with a more recent estimate.

We start with Keynes' "fundamental psychological law" (*General Theory*, Chapter 8) that consumption increases as income increases, but not by as much. Thus

$$c = f(y), \quad \text{with} \quad 0 < \frac{dc}{dy} < 1.$$

Keynes expected the proportion of income consumed to decrease as income increased, and from this follows the argument that redistribution of income in favour of the poor would raise aggregate demand. Further points are (i) that changes in the money value of wealth cause short period changes in the propensity to consume, and (ii) the short-run marginal propensity to consume (m.p.c.) is less than the long-run m.p.c. This latter point follows from the argument that a man's standard of living is inflexible in the short run, discrepancies between his actual income and usual expenditure going straight into savings, for habits require time to adapt to changed circumstances.

These and other statements can be found in Keynes' original specification and several have been used in empirical econometric work. The simplest linear formulation is

$$c = \alpha + \beta y + u,$$

where $\alpha > 0$, $0 < \beta < 1$, and u is a random disturbance term. Here c/y, the share of consumption in income or average propensity to consume (a.p.c.), decreases as income rises. However, this formulation neither distinguishes between short-run and long-run marginal propensities - β is the m.p.c. - nor does it incorporate wealth effects. Also, with this linearisation the redistribution argument is no longer appropriate.

The original rationalisation suggests that the appropriate income variable to use in empirical work is personal disposable income, for it was constructed in terms of an individual deciding his scale of consumption having his net income in mind. Further, the absence of money illusion can be incorporated in this simple linear relation. The saving-consumption decision is assumed independent of the aggregate price level, hence the variables of the consumption function are entered in real rather than nominal terms. So an important first step before estimating such a function from aggregate time series data is to deflate the current values of observed variables by an appropriate price index. This accords with the theoretical specification and, statistically, avoids spuriously overestimating the correlation coefficient. (This can be most easily seen by assuming that we are working with a log-linear equation. Then the true relation is a regression of $\log C$ on $\log Y$, where the aggregate variables C and Y are in constant values. In current values, the variables are (CP) and (YP) where P is a price index, so a regression of $(\log C + \log P)$ on $(\log Y + \log P)$ would be performed, giving a higher R^2 due to the presence of $\log P$ on both sides of the equation.) Similarly, aggregate variables are often expressed in per capita terms, so that the consumption-income relation is not artificially strengthened by the presence of population growth on both sides.

Estimates of the simple linear consumption function

What happened when the simple linear consumption function was estimated by regression methods? A typical result is that given by Davis (1952), using U.S. annual data, 1929-1940, in billions of dollars, deflated for price and population changes:

$$C_t = 11.45 + \underset{(.02)}{0.78}\, Y_t, \qquad R^2 = .986$$

(standard errors in parentheses). However, despite the good fit in the sample period, the relationship consistently underpredicted post-war consumption: ex-post forecasts for 1946-1950 had large negative forecast errors. While a high R^2 does not guarantee good forecasts, doubt is cast on the simple linear formulation by results such as these. Nevertheless a statistical explanation for the poor prediction may be the inappropriate use of ordinary least squares (OLS) estimation methods.

We have shown that simultaneous equation bias results when OLS is applied to structural equations such as

$$C_t = \alpha + \beta Y_t + u_t,$$

by completing the model with $Y_t = C_t + I_t$ and obtaining

$$\text{plim}\,\hat{\beta} = \beta + \frac{(1-\beta)\sigma_u^2}{\sigma_I^2 + \sigma_u^2}. \qquad (\textit{IE}, \text{p.98})$$

The explanatory variable (Y) in the consumption function is not exogenous: it is jointly determined in the two equation system and so is related to the error term in the consumption function, and the simultaneous equation bias results. The second term on the right hand side is seen to be positive, hence $\hat{\beta}$ is upward biased (asymptotically). This problem can be avoided by using a consistent estimator, and since the consumption function here is just-identified, an instrumental variable estimator is appropriate. (It is, of course, identical to the indirect least squares estimator, cf. *IE*, pp. 99-102). Thus it is necessary to compute $b = m_{CI}/m_{YI}$ as a consistent estimate of β.

An example is provided by Haavelmo (1947), using U.S. annual deflated per capita data, 1922-1941. The simple OLS regression of consumers' expenditure on disposable income yields $\hat{\beta} = 0.732$, while the instrumental variable estimate is $b = 0.672$. Thus despite the relatively small number of observations, the positive asymptotic bias in OLS estimates of the consumption function shows through*.

But none of this resolves the post-war forecasting problem: predictions were too low, not too high. A correct estimating procedure would have produced a lower estimate of β and so increased postwar forecasting errors. Hence it became necessary to look for further empirical observations on which tests could be conducted and, more fundamentally, to extend the theory beyond the simple linear relationship.

A second difficulty emerged from other empirical work: the consumption-income ratio proved to be constant over long periods, contradicting the declining share hypothesis. Kuznets (1942) was the first researcher to produce this result, having studied U.S. national income data over the period 1879-1938, during which time national income quadrupled. This appeared to contradict the simple linear specification with $\alpha > 0$. Goldsmith (1955) subsequently confirmed Kuznets' finding for the more relevant aggregate variable, personal income.

Three further empirical points may be noted. First, though long-run time series studies apparently rejected the hypothesis that the consumption-income ratio declines with rising income, nonetheless cross-section (family budget) studies consistently supported the hypothesis. Secondly, cross-section studies continually produced smaller $\hat{\beta}$'s than time series studies. This leads to the suggestion that cross-section estimates could notionally be identified with the short-term, relating to a moment in time. The flatter (lower $\hat{\beta}$) cross-section consumption functions might then move upwards over time, as illustrated in Figure 1. In this way the conflict between cross-section

* Similar results to the ones presented in these two paragraphs are given for the U.K. by Malinvaud (1966, Ch. 4). However I have been unable to reproduce those results using the data in the reference cited (Stone and Rowe, 1956); the data used by Malinvaud appear to be from a source other than that specified.

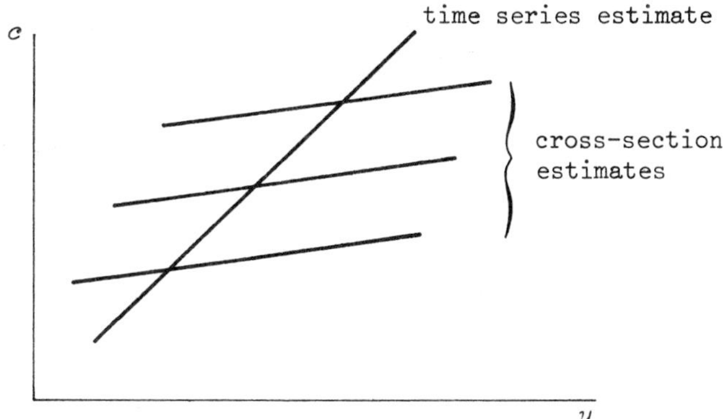

Figure 1

and time series estimates might be resolved in a way consistent with Keynesian theory. Lastly the aggregate consumption-income ratio fluctuated somewhat year by year despite the long-run tendency to constancy. Goldsmith detected cyclical variations in the ratio, which fell during periods of prosperity and rose during recessions, when consumption fell proportionally less than income.

The relative income hypothesis and subsequent developments

Duesenberry (1949) attempted to explain these findings by a re-formulation of consumption theory rather than by statistical methodo-logy. His "relative income" hypothesis has consequences for both cross-section and time-series data. The cross-section effect derives from the hypothesis that a person's consumption behaviour is a function of his position in the income distribution or his "relative income", thus individual consumption behaviour is assumed to be inter-pendent, not independent. The time series effect depends on the idea that consumption behaviour is not readily reversible, and so people react differently to upward and downward income changes rather than having a simple consumption-income relationship equally applicable to income movements in either direction.

The cross-section formulation explains both the constant long-run share of consumption in rising income and the declining share observed in cross-section data. An individual's consumption behaviour is assumed to depend upon his income percentile - he consumes a smaller proportion of his income the higher his percentile position in the income distribution. If all incomes increase by the same proportion, relative incomes and hence consumption's share remain unchanged. Even if one individual moves up to the next income group another must move down because income groups are defined in terms of percentiles. Hence aggregate consumption will remain unchanged. As a simple illustration of the relative income hypothesis, we might express the *i*th household's consumption-income ratio as a function of its relative income:

$$\frac{c_{it}}{y_{it}} = \alpha_0 + \alpha_1 \frac{\bar{y}_t}{y_{it}}$$

where $\bar{y}_t$ is the mean income of the group to which it belongs. Thus with $\alpha_1 > 0$ the share of consumption in income or a.p.c. declines as individual income increases. Equally, writing

$$c_{it} = \alpha_0 y_{it} + \alpha_1 \bar{y}_t$$

we see that at a point in time, the cross-section regression within a group has an m.p.c. equal to α_0, and the function supports the declining share hypothesis, having a positive intercept term $\alpha_1 \bar{y}_t$. On aggregating over both individual households and groups, however, we obtain $C_t = (\alpha_0 + \alpha_1)Y_t$ and the aggregate time series model both yields an m.p.c. of $(\alpha_0 + \alpha_1)$, greater than the cross-section m.p.c., and implies that the share of consumption in income remains constant as income increases over time.

Duesenberry explained the time series effect in terms of prior commitments, habit persistence, and so forth, concluding that "savings at a given level of income, when income is the highest ever attained ... will be higher than savings at a similar income level reached in a decline from a still higher level" (p.89). Thus consumption will be higher than that predicted by the simple linear form when income falls. The consumption-income ratio depends on current income measured relative to the peak previous income, y_t^0 say, and a linear approximation gives

$$c_t = \alpha + \beta_1 y_t + \beta_2 y_t^0$$

where $y_t^0 = \max(y_{t-j})$ for $j \geq 1$.

Then, if income is increasing over time, the peak previous income is always the last period's income, and the simple relationship between consumption and current income at time t has an intercept term $(\alpha + \beta_2 y_{t-1})$. This increases over time, and so the consumption-income relationship moves upwards, as illustrated in Figure 2. The slope of

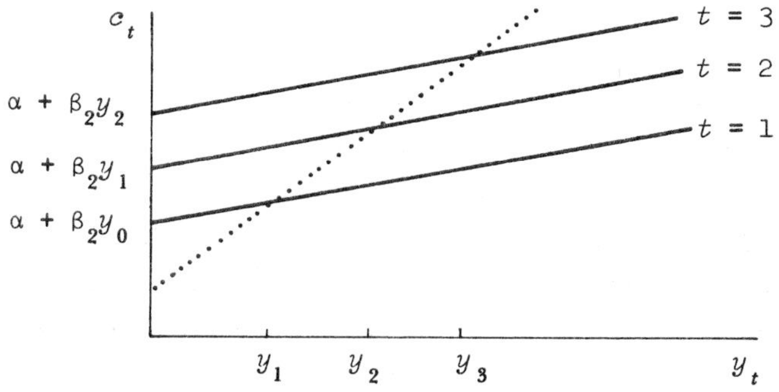

Figure 2

the solid lines is β_1, but in the second period the intercept is $\alpha + \beta_2 y_1$, and so on. If income follows a linear trend, without cyclical fluctuations, $y_t = y_0 + \gamma t$ say, then observations lie along the dotted line in the chart, which has slope $\beta_1 + \beta_2$ and intercept term $\alpha - \beta_2\gamma$: while not necessarily indicating a constant share, this does indicate rather less of a decline. However if income falls, y_t^0 remains unchanged so the intercept does not shift and consumption falls back along one of the flatter 'short-run' consumption functions. This is the so-called ratchet effect.

A precisely equivalent exposition can be given in terms of previous peak consumption (c_t^0) rather than income:

$$c_t^0 = \max(c_{t-j}), \qquad j \geq 1$$

$$c_t = \alpha + \beta_1 y_t + \beta_2 c_t^0.$$

As income, and thereby consumption, increases we can trace out a similar set of short-run functions giving a set of observations along a dotted line. If income falls c_t^0 remains unchanged so consumption falls back along one of the flatter functions.

Brown (1952) suggested that the influence of past habits is continuous in both directions rather than discrete and irreversible. He represented the dependence on past behaviour by putting in the lagged dependent variable rather than the previous peak of income or consumption, so with aggregate time series data we have

$$C_t = \alpha + \beta_1 Y_t + \beta_2 C_{t-1} \qquad 0 < \beta_2 < 1.$$

This modified the Duesenberry pattern of behaviour to give continuous partial adjustment of consumption habits. In the second period of a decline the short-run function relating C_t to Y_t starts to drift back down the diagram again under the Brown hypothesis whereas, according to Duesenberry, consumption always moves back down the same short-run function and this does not shift no matter how rapid the decline in income from the previous peak. This modification of the consumption function obeys the Keynesian requirement that the short-run marginal propensity to consume β_1 is less than the long-run m.p.c. $\beta_1/(1-\beta_2)$, which measures the increase in the equilibrium level of consumption in response to a unit increase in the level of income.

Brown set his consumption function in the context of a small macromodel, and estimated by appropriate simultaneous equations methods. For a two-equation model as used by Haavelmo, with C_{t-1} added to the consumption function, the instrumental variable estimator remains appropriate as long as the error term is non-autocorrelated, which Brown found to be the case. Using annual Canadian data in constant dollars, 1926-1941 and 1946-1949, he reported a short-run m.p.c. of 0.40 and a long-run m.p.c. of 0.59. This seemed rather on the low side, when compared with Kuznets' estimate of the a.p.c. of 0.85-0.88.

Estimates of a similar function, among others, are reported by Evans (1969, §3.3), using annual U.S. data in constant dollars for 1929-1962 (excluding the American war years 1942-1946):

$$C_t = \underset{(.041)}{0.280}\, Y_t + \underset{(.052)}{0.676}\, C_{t-1} .$$

The constant term is suppressed to give a constant a.p.c., in line with the results of Kuznets and Goldsmith. Y_t is personal disposable income and C_t is consumption of nondurables and services: the reasons for excluding durables are discussed below. The estimated m.p.c.'s are short-run: 0.28 and long-run: 0.86, which compares with the a.p.c. for non-durables and services of 0.80. However, simultaneity bias remains in these OLS estimates, and there is evidence of familiar autocorrelation problems.

More recent estimates of this function, which tackle both of these problems, are provided for the U.K. by Hendry (1973), using quarterly data 1957I-1967II. The consumption function for non-durables and services is estimated in the context of an eight-equation macro-model by two stage least squares (*IE*, §5.9) modified to take account of fourth-order autoregressive errors. Seasonally unadjusted deflated data are employed, and the equation is estimated with quarterly dummy variables to represent a seasonally shifting intercept term:

$$C_t = \underset{(.068)}{0.130}\, Y_t + \underset{(.099)}{0.777}\, C_{t-1} + \textit{seasonals}.$$

The corresponding long-run m.p.c. is 0.58, again implying a low income elasticity. This estimate is coincidentally close to Brown's original estimate, although that estimate related to total consumers' expenditure. For Hendry's variables and data period, the corresponding a.p.c. is 0.84.

Note that Evans, following Ball and Drake (1964), calculates long-run m.p.c.'s including an "allowance for growth". The argument for doing so is that the relation between the equilibrium values of consumption and income is calculated more realistically if the equilibrium is a growth path rather than a static position. In the context of the simple model

$$C_t = \alpha + \beta_1 Y_t + \beta_2 C_{t-1}$$

$$Y_t = C_t + I_t$$

the growth would result from growth in I_t. The solution to the final equation for C_t can still be written in the form

$$C_t - C_t^e = \left(\frac{\beta_2}{1-\beta_1}\right)^t (C_0 - C_0^e)$$

(cf. *IE*, §3.2 and Ex. 3.1) so that stability is assessed in the usual way, but the equilibrium value C_t^e is now a function of t. The behaviour of this equilibrium value is the same as that of I_t: if I_t has a constant value I, then C_t^e is constant and we have a static equilibrium; if I_t grows exponentially, $I_t = \lambda^t I_0$, $\lambda > 1$, then so does C_t^e (also Y_t^e). The relation between the equilibrium values of consumption and income is then obtained by substituting C_t/λ for C_{t-1}, whereupon the long-run m.p.c. is

$$\frac{\beta_1}{1-\beta_2/\lambda} = \frac{\lambda\beta_1}{\lambda-\beta_2} .$$

The previous simpler case obtains when $\lambda = 1$; if $\lambda > 1$ the long-run m.p.c. is smaller. In practice few dramatic changes result given the usual order of magnitude of λ: Evans takes $\lambda = 1.02$, corresponding to 2% growth per annum, whereupon the long-run m.p.c. is estimated from the above results as 0.83, compared with 0.86 when $\lambda = 1$.

Brown's introduction of the lagged dependent variable in the consumption function is of course equivalent to putting in an infinite distributed lag in income with geometrically declining weights. The estimated equation is then obtained by a Koyck transformation (*IE*, p.33), and the following formulations are equivalent:

$$C_t = \frac{\alpha}{1-\beta_2} + \beta_1 \sum_{j=0}^{\infty} \beta_2^j Y_{t-j}$$

$$C_t = \alpha + \beta_1 Y_t + \beta_2 C_{t-1} .$$

This point was not originally noted by Brown but Koyck's work came somewhat later. We shall see below that there is a relationship between such models and the form in which the permanent income hypothesis is tested with aggregate time series data. This concludes our comments on the addition of dynamic behaviour to the over-simple form in which Keynesian theory had originally been tested.

The permanent income hypothesis

The major subsequent contribution was due to Friedman (1957), whose permanent income hypothesis provides an explanation for some of the statistical phenomena noted above.

Friedman's hypothesis is that the consumer disregards fortuitous variations in income when drawing up consumption plans; he considers only his expected, 'normal', or permanent income (y_P). This is defined as the amount that the consumer unit believes it can consume whilst maintaining its wealth intact. The discrepancy between observed current or measured income (y) and y_P is described as transitory income (y_T): $y = y_P + y_T$. Consumption is likewise divided into permanent or planned (c_P) and transitory (c_T) components: $c = c_P + c_T$. Friedman includes an allowance for services derived from stocks of durable goods in the definition of c_P and treats purchases of durables as investment.

In drawing up its consumption plans the consumer unit only has in mind its permanent income, and the ratio of permanent consumption to permanent income is independent of y_P:

$$c_P = ky_P .$$

Thus Friedman's consumption function has no intercept term, with the consequence that the lr m.p.c. (k) is equal to the a.p.c. in accordance with the Kuznets-Goldsmith type of evidence. k may in turn depend upon various factors such as the individual's discount rate, his portfolio of assets, tastes, and demographic factors (age, household composition, etc.). The elasticity of c_P with respect to y_P in this framework is 1.

To complete the statistical specification of the model Friedman assumes that

(i) the transitory components have zero means:

$$E(y_T) = E(c_T) = 0,$$

(ii) the covariances between the permanent components and the corresponding transitory components are zero:

$$\text{cov}(c_P, c_T) = \text{cov}(y_P, y_T) = 0,$$

(iii) the transitory components of income and consumption are uncorrelated with one another:

$$\text{cov}(c_T, y_T) = 0.$$

This is one of the stronger assumptions for $E(c_T y_T) = 0$ implies that a windfall gain will be saved (in the Friedman sense of not being spent on non-durable goods): a positive value for y_T will not lead to a deviation from the consumption plan.

This specification of the consumption function turns out to be that of the classical statistical "errors in variables" model. The true variables obey an exact functional relationship, but they are observed with error. The result is that least squares estimation of $c_P = ky_P$ using the observed variables c and y gives an inconsistent estimate of k. This situation provides yet another example of bias in least squares estimates of consumption functions, and a further possible explanation of the least squares results. Observed consumption c is given by

$$c = c_P + c_T = ky_P + c_T$$

and is thus related to observed income as follows

$$c = ky + (c_T - ky_T).$$

This gives a linear relationship between the observed variables together with an error term $(c_T - ky_T)$, which is itself a function of the two transitory components. So this equation does not obey the requirement of the classical least squares regression model: the explanatory variable is not independent of the error term, though for a slightly different reason than we have met so far. (Previous cases were those of an explanatory endogenous variable being correlated with the error term giving rise to simultaneous equations bias, and the lagged dependent variable-autocorrelated error problem). Here the explanatory variable y has a transitory component which also appears in the error term, so they have a non-zero covariance and the least squares estimate will not be consistent. Let us now examine the nature of this bias.

Suppose that we have data $\{c_i, y_i\}$ for a sample of time periods or households and we calculate the familiar least squares estimate $(\hat{\beta})$ of the marginal propensity to consume, which is k in this case:

$$\hat{\beta} = \frac{\Sigma(c_i-\bar{c})(y_i-\bar{y})}{\Sigma(y_i-\bar{y})^2} .$$

Following the usual procedure of examining the effect of our statistical assumptions by substituting in for the dependent variable c, and separating components, we have

$$\hat{\beta} = \frac{\Sigma\{k(y_{Pi}-\bar{y}_P)+c_{Ti}-\bar{c}_T\}\{y_{Pi}-\bar{y}_P+y_{Ti}-\bar{y}_T\}}{\Sigma(y_{Pi}-\bar{y}_P+y_{Ti}-\bar{y}_T)^2} .$$

Ideally we would like to evaluate the expected value of this quantity. But we cannot do so for a finite sample because as usual the expected value of the ratio is not equal to the ratio of the expected values of the top and bottom taken separately. Therefore we must resort to probability limits and derive large sample results. Multiplying out in the numerator and denominator gives

$$\hat{\beta} = \frac{\Sigma\{k(y_{Pi}-\bar{y}_P)^2+k(y_{Pi}-\bar{y}_P)(y_{Ti}-\bar{y}_T)+(c_{Ti}-\bar{c}_T)(y_{Pi}-\bar{y}_P)+(c_{Ti}-\bar{c}_T)(y_{Ti}-\bar{y}_T)\}}{\Sigma\{(y_{Pi}-\bar{y}_P)^2+(y_{Ti}-\bar{y}_T)^2+2(y_{Pi}-\bar{y}_P)(y_{Ti}-\bar{y}_T)\}}$$

Now we divide top and bottom by the sample size so that the resulting quantities are estimates of the covariances about which we have just made assumptions. The estimated covariances in the last three terms in the numerator and the last term in the denominator all have zero expected value by the assumptions (ii) and (iii) above. (The third term in the numerator requires the substitution of $\frac{1}{k}c_P$ for y_P before the application of assumption (ii).) The remaining terms give the variances of the permanent and transitory income components, so the probability limit of the least squares coefficient estimate in the simple Keynesian consumption function is given by

$$\text{plim } \hat{\beta} = k \frac{\text{var}(y_P)}{\text{var}(y_P)+\text{var}(y_T)} = k \frac{\text{var}(y_P)}{\text{var}(y)} .$$

The result is that $\hat{\beta}$ is not an unbiased estimate of k, even asymptotically. The probability limit of $\hat{\beta}$ will be rather less than k because

$$\frac{\text{var}(y_P)}{\text{var}(y_P)+\text{var}(y_T)} < 1.$$

So the m.p.c. tends to be underestimated by the simple linear regression coefficient, the more so the greater the relative variance of transitory income.

Similarly the estimated income elasticity of consumption will be less than one. Evaluating at the point of sample means

$$\eta_{cy} = \hat{\beta} \frac{\bar{y}}{\bar{c}} = \hat{\beta} \frac{1}{\text{apc}} .$$

Now k is consistently estimated as $\frac{\bar{c}}{\bar{y}}$, the average propensity to consume. (To see this, write $\hat{k} = \frac{1}{n}\Sigma c_i / \frac{1}{n}\Sigma y_i$. The expected value of the top is k times the expected value of the bottom, $E(y_P)$, using assumption (i) and $c_P = ky_P$. The variances of the top and bottom are all of the form σ^2/n, and so go to zero as $n \to \infty$ (we have tended to assume that this requirement is met in calculating probability limits, but strictly it should always be checked, cf. *IE*, p.76). Thus the plim of the top is k times the plim of the bottom, and plim $(\hat{k}) = k$.) Hence if η_{cy} is the estimated elasticity of permanent components based on the least squares coefficient $\hat{\beta}$, we have

$$\text{plim } \eta_{cy} = \text{plim } \hat{\beta} \frac{\bar{y}}{\bar{c}} = k \frac{\text{var } y_P}{\text{var } y} \frac{1}{k} = \frac{\text{var } y_P}{\text{var } y} < 1,$$

thus plim η_{cy} is less than the value of one given by the Friedman model.

So far we have said nothing about whether the data used in the exercise are from cross-section or time series samples: the results hold for both. With cross-section data, one would expect that the least squares estimate of the m.p.c. for a group whose income contains a relatively important y_T would be smaller than that of other groups. Friedman examined farm families in this light - their observed incomes are more variable, with the transitory component contributing relatively more to the total variation. He therefore expected to find that their 'apparent' or estimated $\hat{\beta}\overline{y}/\overline{c}$ would be less than that of non-farm families, and the hypothesis was corroborated. Similarly cross-section income elasticity estimates for different years show the lowest values for the war year 1944 when the transitory component was relatively important, as would be expected in an unsettled period.

Applying the preceding arguments to time series data, the hypothesis suggests that the m.p.c. estimated by simple regression will be lower for shorter data periods, when there is less secular change in income and so smaller variation in the permanent component, and Friedman found that this was the case. The hypothesis suggests no generalisation about the relation between time series and cross-section estimates, both depending on the income structure in the sample. Nevertheless it is not surprising that the above time series estimate for 1929-1940, a period of stagnation and sharp short-period movements, is rather lower not only than estimates for other periods but also than estimates obtained from budget studies. Having criticised the simple regression formulation for time series data, Friedman then turned to an alternative procedure.

Aggregate time series estimates under the permanent income hypothesis

To estimate the aggregate consumption function $C_{Pt} = kY_{Pt}$ we need series on the two variables. Where are they to be found? Taking planned consumption first, consumption of non-durables and services is usually used directly. The reasons for doing so relate to Friedman's original delineation of the relevant decision to be considered in consumption theory, and the treating of expenditure on durable goods as investment. In any case, the error in the dependent variable is not the source of the difficulty discussed above. The inconsistency in OLS estimates results only from the error in the explanatory variable, and transitory consumption plays no part in the argument. In fact we could not distinguish between a measurement error in the dependent variable and the conventional disturbance term representing the influence of omitted variables.

How do we estimate permanent income? Friedman employed expected income using the adaptive expectations hypothesis that Cagan had applied a year earlier in his work on hyperinflation (cf. *IE*, pp. 34-35). It is often written in the following continuous formulation:

$$Y_{Pt} = \beta \int_0^\infty e^{-(\beta - |\alpha|)l} \; Y_{t-l} \, dl.$$

One slight departure from Cagan is the inclusion of α, a growth effect. If it is deleted (i.e. set α=0) the resulting expression can be obtained as the solution to a differential equation adaptive expectations model. This has permanent income responding to discrepancies between current and permanent income:

$$\frac{dY_{Pt}}{dt} = \beta(Y_t - Y_{Pt}),$$

and permanent or expected normal income is itself given by the exponentially weighted moving average type of expression represented by the above integral. Friedman then constructed a discrete time approximation to this hypothesis, having only annual data. This estimates permanent income as a distributed lag function of current and past incomes with geometrically declining weights, and a further approximation is to truncate the lag function after the first seventeen terms:

$$\hat{Y}_{Pt} = (1-\gamma) \sum_{j=0}^{16} \gamma^j Y_{t-j} .$$

For estimation purposes Friedman constructed a number of $\hat{Y}_{Pt}$ series, using different values for γ in each case, ran the consumption function regressions, (using data in real, per capita terms) and chose that value of γ which produced the highest R^2. The best estimates of the linear relation between C_t and $\hat{Y}_{Pt}$ produced a t-ratio for the intercept term of 0.24, which was accepted as support for the hypothesis of a proportional relationship $C_{Pt} = kY_{Pt}$. k was estimated at 0.88, which was quite close to the observed average propensity to consume $\overline{C}/\overline{Y}$, (which provides a consistent estimate of k). The estimate of the distributed lag coefficients implied an average lag of $2\frac{1}{2}$ years.

Of course it is not necessary to truncate the above distributed lag function at all. We can replace it by an infinite distributed lag and apply a Koyck transformation (*IE*, p.33) to get

$$C_t = \gamma C_{t-1} + k(1-\gamma)Y_t .$$

This is almost identical to the form used by Brown. Hence with time series data Friedman provided a new interpretation of Brown's equation, with the significant difference that the constant term was suppressed. (This modification was adopted in Evans' results reported above.) Thus once one chooses to estimate permanent income as a weighted average of past observed incomes the permanent income hypothesis for time series data is scarcely distinguishable from other hypotheses, and all of them require attention to be paid to simultaneity problems.

Liviatan's tests of the permanent income hypothesis

Liviatan (1963) has cross-section data on urban families in Israel, each of which was interviewed in two consecutive years ("panel" data). Essentially he would like to relate estimated m.p.c.'s to the variability of income which, according to the permanent income hypothesis, is the source of the downward bias. However a direct attack on this is not possible, because two years' data do not provide an adequate measure of income variability.

First, to give the flavour of his argument consider what would happen if one estimated the simple linear consumption function in first differences. Observed consumption is given by $c = ky + (c_T - ky_T)$. Using the two years' data to express the equation in first difference form, we would expect to obtain much lower estimates of the m.p.c., for y_P is stable over time and so changes in y are largely due to temporary components, which do not affect consumption. Let us look at this argument more closely. For each family the changes in consumption and income, Δc and Δy, are calculated, and the coefficient in a simple regression employing these variables, which we denote $\hat{\beta}_\Delta$ is

$$\hat{\beta}_\Delta = \frac{\Sigma \Delta c_i \Delta y_i}{\Sigma(\Delta y_i)^2} .$$

By the same procedure as before (p.13-14), with a slight extension of assumptions (ii) and (iii) so that they give zero covariances between components in <u>any</u> time period, we obtain

$$\text{plim } \hat{\beta}_\Delta = k \frac{\text{var}\Delta y_P}{\text{var}\Delta y} = k \frac{\text{var}(y_{P2}-y_{P1})}{\text{var}(y_2-y_1)} ,$$

using the subscripts 1 and 2 to denote the two years of the study. (Note that in general these two years need not be consecutive, although in Liviatan's case they are.) Multiplying out, this gives

$$\text{plim } \hat{\beta}_\Delta = k \frac{\text{var } y_{P2}+\text{var } y_{P1}-2\text{cov}(y_{P1},y_{P2})}{\text{var } y_{P2}+\text{var } y_{P1}-2\text{cov}(y_{P1},y_{P2})+\text{var } y_{T2}+\text{var } y_{T1}} ,$$

having additionally assumed that the covariance between y_{T1} and y_{T2} which features in the denominator is zero. So, assuming equal variances in the two years, and dividing top and bottom by 2, we need to compare

$$\text{plim } \hat{\beta}_\Delta = k \frac{\text{var } y_P-\text{cov}(y_{P1},y_{P2})}{\text{var } y_P+\text{var } y_T-\text{cov}(y_{P1},y_{P2})} \quad \text{with} \quad \text{plim } \hat{\beta} = k \frac{\text{var } y_P}{\text{var } y_P+\text{var } y_T} .$$

The permanent components in the two years will be positively correlated, indeed Friedman assumes that they will be highly correlated. Subtracting the same quantity from the top and bottom of a ratio reduces its value ($0 < \frac{a}{b} < 1$ and $0 < c < b$ imply $\frac{a-c}{b-c} < \frac{a}{b}$) so we have plim $\hat{\beta}_\Delta$ < plim $\hat{\beta}$. Thus under the permanent income hypothesis we expect to find $\hat{\beta}_\Delta < \hat{\beta}$, whereas with the linear Keynesian consumption function, we expect no systematic difference.

It turns out that $\hat{\beta}_\Delta$ is smaller than $\hat{\beta}$, but not substantially so, which is rather unfavourable to the permanent income hypothesis. Unfortunately, to carry out this test of the hypothesis, additional assumptions have been made (that the correlation between successive values of the income components is high for y_P and zero for y_T) and it is not clear in such a situation whether the basic hypothesis or the additional assumptions are at fault. A further possible explanation is that the data are from a savings survey rather than an expenditure survey, and any measurement error in income is automatically transmitted to the estimate of consumption. Suppose

$$\text{observed } y = y_P + y_T + e.$$

Then consumption is estimated as observed income less observed savings,

$$\text{i.e. estimated } c = y - s = c_P + c_T + e,$$

which has an error equal to that in observed income. Such common errors would increase the covariance between the two observed income and consumption series, the data apparently negating the assumption that c_T and y_T are uncorrelated when it is in fact true. Consequently Liviatan turns to methods which attempt to eliminate the influence of errors in the observed variables.

Instrumental variable estimation of k

Our previous encounter with the instrumental variable (IV) method was in the context of simultaneous equation estimation (*IE*, §5.7), where the explanatory variable on the right hand side of a regression equation was correlated with the error term, because it was an endogenous variable. The problem here is similar: the explanatory variable y is related to the error term, since both contain y_T. Hence we require an instrumental variable z correlated with y_P but not related to the error term $(c_T - ky_T)$. Then the IV estimate of the m.p.c., b say, will be

$$b = \frac{\Sigma(c_i-\bar{c})(z_i-\bar{z})}{\Sigma(y_i-\bar{y})(z_i-\bar{z})} .$$

If z is correlated with y_P but is independent of c_T and y_T, then b is a consistent estimate of k:

$$\text{plim } b = \text{plim } \frac{\Sigma\{k(y_{Pi}-\bar{y}_P)+(c_{Ti}-\bar{c}_T)\}(z_i-\bar{z})}{\Sigma\{(y_{Pi}-\bar{y}_P)+(y_{Ti}-\bar{y}_T)\}(z_i\ \bar{z})} = k.$$

If the least squares coefficient $\hat{\beta}$ (which is expected to be downward biased under the permanent income hypothesis) is substantially below b (which is expected to be unbiased) we shall have found corroborative evidence in favour of the hypothesis. But what variable in the model can be used as an appropriate instrument?

Liviatan first suggests income in the 'other' of his two years, y^* say. This procedure is all right if the transitory components in the two years are uncorrelated, so that the instrumental variable is then independent of the error term. Doing this for each of the two years, and for each of two sub-groups of his sample (employees and self-employed), Liviatan finds two highly significant differences between $\hat{\beta}$ and b, which support the permanent income hypothesis, and two which do not. But even in the favourable cases the estimated income elasticity remains less than one.

But what would be the effect of a (serial) correlation between the two transitory components? In some of his earlier work Friedman suggested that the consumer's horizon was more than two years, so that Liviatan's data may include sub-periods of the same planning period, whereupon y_{T1} and y_{T2} will not be independent. Positive correlation between the transitory components produces another downward bias in b. Denoting the income for the year in question by y, and the other year's income, used as an instrumental variable, by y^*, and retaining the assumption of independence of permanent and transitory components in any year, the above equation becomes

$$\text{plim } b = \text{plim } \frac{k\Sigma(y_{Pi}-\bar{y}_P)(y^*_{Pi}-\bar{y}^*_P)}{\Sigma\{(y_{Pi}-\bar{y}_P)(y^*_{Pi}-\bar{y}^*_P)+(y_{Ti}-\bar{y}_T)(y^*_{Ti}-\bar{y}^*_T)\}} .$$

Hence, if there is positive correlation between the transitory components the denominator is increased and plim $b < k$. This could account for the two non-significant differences between $\hat{\beta}$ and b and for $\eta_{cy} < 1$.

Is there another instrumental variable to hand? The other year's consumption, c^*, will provide a consistent estimate again if the transitory components are uncorrelated. What if c_T and c^*_T are positively correlated? It turns out that in this case b will be upwards biased:

$$b = \frac{\Sigma(c_i-\bar{c})(c^*_i-\bar{c}^*)}{\Sigma(y_i-\bar{y})(c^*_i-\bar{c}^*)} = \frac{\Sigma\{k(y_i-\bar{y})+c_{Ti}-\bar{c}_T-k(y_{Ti}-\bar{y}_T)\}(c^*_i-\bar{c}^*)}{\Sigma(y_i-\bar{y})(c^*_i-\bar{c}^*)}$$

$$= k + \frac{\Sigma\{c_{Ti}-\bar{c}_T-k(y_{Ti}-\bar{y}_T)\}\{c^*_{Pi}-\bar{c}^*_P + c^*_{Ti}-\bar{c}^*_T\}}{\Sigma(y_i-\bar{y})(c^*_i-\bar{c}^*)} .$$

Under the usual assumptions about the transitory components and serial independence of c_T, plim $b = k$ as before. But if $\text{cov}(c_T,c^*_T)>0$ then plim $b > k$. So if the calculated b is still less than the a.p.c., or the estimated elasticity is still less than one, despite this upward bias, this will contradict the permanent income hypothesis. Now if durables are included in consumption expenditures, there may be negative correlation between transitory components, as Friedman comments, for a positive discrepancy from planned purchases of durables this year might be associated with a negative discrepancy next year. Indeed Liviatan does get higher estimates of b when durables are excluded. But even then, Liviatan finds that b is less than the a.p.c., despite the upward bias, and so Friedman's model is contradicted by the data. In his reply, Friedman appraises the findings cautiously: "If these results should be confirmed for other bodies of data, they would constitute relevant and significant evidence that the elasticity of permanent components is less than unity."

The role of liquid assets

We conclude our brief look at consumption function estimation with a more recent aggregate time series study, which incorporates a real balance effect. Wealth was mentioned as a possible determinant of consumption in the original Keynesian specification, and in recent years its inclusion has been associated with the Quantity Theory. However its role has remained to counterbalance changing income streams over long periods. In estimation, liquid assets rather than total wealth have come into use for two reasons. On the one hand they can be more reliably measured than wealth, and so may be used as a proxy variable for wealth, but more significantly, it is argued that liquid assets are the more relevant element of wealth to be included.

Evidence for the latter view is provided by an aggregate time series study by Zellner, Huang, and Chau (1965). Here a real balance effect is included in the consumption function so that any imbalance in the consumer's liquid assets position affects his consumption behaviour. If liquid assets are sufficient with respect to some desired position, consumption plans will be carried out, but if they are insufficient, expenditures will be reduced. Also, the study follows Friedman in using expected income (estimated permanent income) as the appropriate income variable. The consumption function is given as

$$C_t = kY_t^e + \alpha(L_{t-1} - L_t^d) + u_t,$$

where L_{t-1} represents real liquid asset holdings at the start of the period, L_t^d the desired level for the current period, and $\alpha > 0$. Estimated permanent income is given by

$$Y_t^e = (1-\gamma) \sum_0^\infty \gamma^j Y_{t-j} ,$$

and L_t^d is assumed to be in direct proportion,

$$L_t^d = \eta Y_t^e,$$

"in accord with Friedman's view of one of the main determinants of the demand for money." After a Koyck transformation, the final equation is obtained as

$$C_t = \gamma C_{t-1} + \alpha L_{t-1} - \alpha\gamma L_{t-2} + (k-\alpha\eta)(1-\gamma)Y_t + u_t - \gamma u_{t-1} \,.$$

Although there are four regression coefficients and four parameters, the equation has a mixture of under- and over-identified parameters. It is not possible to separate out k and η, but α and γ are over-identified, so it is necessary to impose the requirement that the coefficient of L_{t-2} is minus the product of the coefficients of C_{t-1} and L_{t-1} : this entails a non-linear estimation procedure. The final equation's error term,

$$v_t = u_t - \gamma u_{t-1} \,,$$

is a first-order moving average of the original disturbance term, and is autocorrelated even if u_t is not. As a first approximation, Zellner, Huang, and Chau assume that v_t follows a first-order autoregression:

$$v_t = \rho v_{t-1} + \varepsilon_t \,.$$

Simultaneity problems are also present, and so the two stage least squares method is employed, modified to take account of the two above-mentioned complications. (In fact the interest rate is also added as a determinant of L_t^d, but its parameter estimate is not significantly different from zero.) Using U.S. quarterly data, 1947 IV - 1961 II, in constant dollar per capita terms, with C_t being total personal consumption expenditures, the model performs quite well. The estimate of γ is 0.873, implying an average lag of 6.9 quarters, somewhat smaller than Friedman's estimate of 2½ years. The hypothesis that imbalances in liquid asset holdings exert an influence on consumers' expenditure is supported by the estimate of α of 0.697, with a standard error of 0.153. If η is assigned the value of 0.764, the sample average ratio of liquid assets to income, then from the estimate of $(k-\alpha\eta)$ the very reasonable value $\hat{k} = 0.937$

results. Finally although the autoregressive error is only an approximation, and the occurrence of the same parameter in the moving average error and the regression coefficients is ignored, the estimate of ρ of -0.321 (s.e. 0.124) is in accordance with the original specification. That is, this negative value supports the expectations formulation as against alternatives such as partial adjustment hypotheses.

Chapter 2

THE PRODUCTION FUNCTION

Introduction

We begin our case study of production functions with a brief review of the relevant economic theory. The traditional theory begins with two inputs (K and L) which are continuously variable and continuously substitutable in production at all times; to each combination there corresponds a unique maximum quantity of output:

$$Q = F(K,L).$$

This takes us away from the realm of linear production models with fixed coefficients. In effect the function is regarded as a technical relation in flow terms, flows of services from stocks of labour and capital combining to produce a flow of output. The function summarises the efficient production possibilities open to a firm, a technical maximization problem having been solved.

It is conventional to differentiate between capital and labour inputs, but the above representation in terms of only two inputs is a gross over-simplification, for there are of course many varieties of capital and labour inputs. These can be combined into single aggregate variables provided that the marginal rate of substitution between any two kinds of one factor is independent of any variety of the other factor, and these aggregate variables can be treated as if they were actual individual inputs provided that they are linear homogeneous functions of the different varieties. (We shall remind ourselves of these technical terms in a moment.) Thus an aggregation problem arises even at the level of an individual firm, long before the question of the aggregation of equations in industry studies arises - it is only avoided at the extreme micro level of one man with one machine. In practice we tend to make the heroic assumption that the above necessary conditions are satisfied more often than we acknowledge heterogeneity by introducing sub-categories of K and L as subsidiary arguments in the production function.

At first we shall assume the function to be fixed although in due course we shall allow it to shift in some way, for example, due to (disembodied) technical change. This poses a problem of distinguishing movements along a given production function from shifts of the function, which is the basic problem in estimating technical progress. Since the production function is a mere summary of technical constraints, by itself it allows for no testing of economic hypotheses. Actual observed data are the results of economic decisions in which the production function is but one constraint. Thus production functions are used in conjunction with marginal productivity theory to provide explanations of factor prices and the levels of factor utilization, and so at a theoretical level play a central role in the analysis of growth and distribution. This analysis is discussed at the macro level, while at the micro level problems of substitution possibilities and economies of scale arise. The data which are available correspond to reduced form observations and raise familiar identification problems, for the production function is embedded in a simultaneous equations model - it cannot be identified if, for example, the marginal productivity conditions are not distinguishable from it. We shall be treating situations in which economic agents are assumed to have solved their technical problems, and examine inputs, outputs, prices and so on making various assumptions about the nature of the economic system in which the firm or entrepreneur operates. The questions that have been most frequently addressed to the data that result from this process concern the extent of economies of scale, substitutability of factors, and technical progress.

Properties of the neoclassical production function

The production function $Q = F(K,L)$ is single-valued, continuous, and (at least) twice differentiable. Writing

$$\frac{\partial Q}{\partial K} = F_K, \quad \frac{\partial^2 Q}{\partial K^2} = F_{KK},$$

and so forth, we require

$$F_K > 0, \quad F_L > 0, \quad F_{KK} < 0, \quad F_{LL} < 0$$

ensuring marginal products which are positive and decreasing. Suppose capital and labour inputs are increased in some proportion h, then Q may increase in the same proportion, or by some larger or smaller proportion,

$$\text{i.e.} \quad F(hK,hL) = h^n F(K,L) = h^n Q.$$

n is a parameter in which we shall be interested, as it gives the degree of homogeneity of the function. A value of n=1 indicates constant returns to scale, and increasing or decreasing returns are indicated by values greater than or less than unity. An important property of homogeneous functions is given by Euler's theorem, which says that the sum of the first partial derivates weighted by the quantity of the factor is equal to output times the degree of homogeneity,

$$F_K K + F_L L = nQ.$$

As an illustration take the case of n=1, namely, a "linear, homogeneous" production function, exhibiting constant returns to scale. Then

$$F_K K + F_L L = Q$$

so if factors are paid their marginal products the product is exhausted: there will be no pure losses or profits. (Euler's theorem also features in consumer demand functions which are often made homogeneous of degree zero in income and prices to ensure no money illusion: if incomes and prices are increased by the same proportion consumption remains unaffected.) The linear homogeneous case can be written in per capita terms as a function of one variable. Setting $h = \frac{1}{L}$, we have

$$\frac{Q}{L} = F(\frac{K}{L},\frac{L}{L}).$$

If we define $q = \frac{Q}{L}$ = output per capita and $k = \frac{K}{L}$ = the capital-labour ratio then this function can be written

$$q = f(k).$$

It can be represented as follows

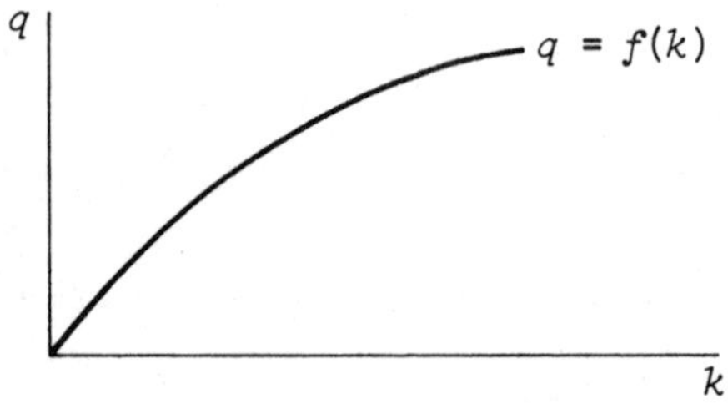

Figure 3

where $\frac{dq}{dk} > 0$, $\frac{d^2q}{dk^2} < 0$.

An isoquant diagram shows the function $Q = F(K,L)$ for given levels of output.

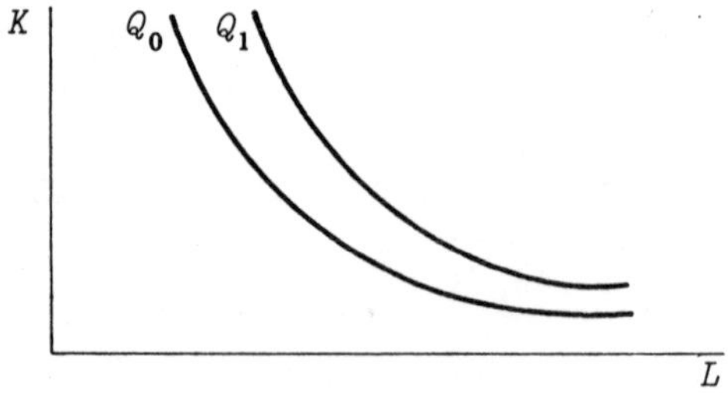

Figure 4

Taking the total derivative of $F(K,L)$ = constant gives

$$dQ = F_K dK + F_L dL = 0 \text{ along an isoquant.}$$

Output does not change as we move along an isoquant, hence the absolute value of the slope of the isoquant, the marginal rate of substitution R, is given by

$$R = -\frac{dK}{dL} = \frac{F_L}{F_K}.$$

This is assumed to decrease as substitution proceeds giving an isoquant convex to the origin. The elasticity of substitution (σ) is a further parameter of interest. It is defined as the proportionate change in the factor-input ratio as a result of a proportionate change in the marginal rate of substitution, and measures the ease of substitution between factors.

$$\sigma = \frac{d \log (K/L)}{d \log R} > 0.$$

A value of zero indicates that no substitution is possible - factors are combined in a fixed proportion.

The Cobb-Douglas production function

The Cobb-Douglas production function provides a convenient and widely-used illustration. We have

$$Q = AK^{\alpha}L^{\beta}.$$

The degree of homogeneity is $\alpha + \beta$ since

$$F(hK,hL) = A(hK)^{\alpha}(hL)^{\beta} = h^{\alpha+\beta}AK^{\alpha}L^{\beta} = h^{\alpha+\beta}Q.$$

Hence the Cobb-Douglas has constant returns to scale when $n = \alpha+\beta = 1$. (In that case $q = Ak^{\alpha}$ where $q = \frac{Q}{L}$, $k = \frac{K}{L}$.) The marginal products are obtained by differentation:

$$\frac{\partial Q}{\partial K} = \alpha AK^{\alpha-1}L^{\beta} = \alpha(\frac{Q}{K}).$$

Thus the elasticity of output with respect to capital is α and the marginal product of capital diminishes with increasing k if $\alpha < 1$. Similarly

$$\frac{\partial Q}{\partial L} = \beta A K^{\alpha} L^{\beta-1} = \beta\left(\frac{Q}{L}\right).$$

The marginal rate of substitution of K for L is

$$R = \frac{\partial Q}{\partial L} \Big/ \frac{\partial Q}{\partial K} = \beta\frac{Q}{L} \Big/ \alpha\frac{Q}{K} = \frac{\beta}{\alpha}\frac{K}{L}.$$

To derive the elasticity of substitution we can write this equation as

$$\log (R) = \log\left(\frac{\beta}{\alpha}\right) + \log\left(\frac{K}{L}\right),$$

hence

$$\sigma = \frac{d \log (K/L)}{d \log R} = 1.$$

The economic model

Now let us examine a simple economic model which incorporates a production function. The technical relation is one constraint embedded in a model of firm behaviour and the observed values of prices, capital, labour and output are generated by a set of simultaneous relationships. Hence capital and labour cannot be treated as exogenous variables determining output in a single relationship - they are jointly determined. The simplest case is given by assuming perfect competition in both factor and product markets, which means that prices of output (p), capital (r) and labour (w) are predetermined - the firm is a price-taker.

We first look at the cost-minimisation problem, as we shall shortly be examining a cost function study. For a given level of output Q, determined exogenously by demand conditions, say, the firm must choose its input levels K and L so as to minimise total costs

$$TC = rK + wL$$

subject to $Q = F(K,L)$. The Lagrangean is

$$\mathcal{L} = rK + wL - \lambda\{Q-F(K,L)\}.$$

The first order conditions are

$$\frac{\partial \mathcal{L}}{\partial K} = r + \lambda F_K = 0$$

$$\frac{\partial \mathcal{L}}{\partial L} = w + \lambda F_L = 0$$

so $$\frac{F_L}{F_K} = \frac{w}{r},$$

and $$\frac{\partial \mathcal{L}}{\partial \lambda} = 0 \qquad \text{so} \qquad Q = F(K,L).$$

Thus the optimal solution occurs when the marginal rate of substitution is equal to the factor price ratio, and in this context (cost-minimising price-takers) the elasticity of substitution is given as

$$\sigma = \frac{d\ \log(K/L)}{d\ \log(w/r)},$$

the percentage change in the capital-labour ratio in response to a one percent change in the factor price ratio. Solving the above two conditions gives the cost-minimising input levels in terms of their prices and the given output level. Substituting these into the expression for TC gives the minimum cost function, or just the cost function (the dual of the production function) in terms of r, w, and Q.

Example

For the Cobb-Douglas production function

$$Q = AK^{\alpha}L^{\beta}$$

we have

$$\frac{F_L}{F_K} = \frac{\beta}{\alpha}\frac{K}{L} = \frac{w}{r}.$$

From this we obtain

$$L = \frac{\beta}{\alpha}\frac{r}{w}K$$

and substituting into the production function gives

$$Q = A\ K^{\alpha+\beta}\left(\frac{\beta}{\alpha}\frac{r}{w}\right)^{\beta}$$

which on rearranging yields the cost-minimising input function,

$$K = \left(\frac{Q}{A}\right)^{1/n}\left(\frac{\beta}{\alpha}\frac{r}{w}\right)^{-\beta/n}$$

where $n = \alpha+\beta$ is the degree of returns to scale. Similarly, for labour input:

$$L = \left(\frac{Q}{A}\right)^{1/n}\left(\frac{\alpha}{\beta}\frac{w}{r}\right)^{-\alpha/n}$$

The cost function is then obtained as follows:

$$\begin{aligned} TC &= rK + wL \\ &= \left(\frac{Q}{A}\right)^{1/n}\{r\left(\frac{\beta}{\alpha}\frac{r}{w}\right)^{-\beta/n} + w\left(\frac{\alpha}{\beta}\frac{w}{r}\right)^{-\alpha/n}\}, \end{aligned}$$

$$TC = k\, Q^{1/n}\, r^{\alpha/n}\, w^{\beta/n},$$

where the constant k is given by

$$\begin{aligned} k &= A^{-1/n} \{\alpha^{\beta/n}\, \beta^{-\beta/n} + \alpha^{-\alpha/n}\, \beta^{\alpha/n}\} \\ &= A^{-1/n} (\alpha+\beta)(\alpha^{\alpha}\beta^{\beta})^{-1/n} \\ &= n(A\alpha^{\alpha}\beta^{\beta})^{-1/n} \end{aligned}$$

Thus the cost function is log-linear in output and factor prices:

$$\log TC = \log k + \frac{1}{n}\log Q + \frac{\alpha}{n}\log r + \frac{\beta}{n}\log w.$$

The profit maximisation problem is to choose the levels of output and inputs which maximise profits. Since costs must be minimised if profits are to be maximised, the problem is simply to maximise

$$\Pi = pQ - TC(Q,r,w)$$

with respect to Q - there is no constraint as the production function is incorporated in the derivation of TC. The first order condition $\partial\Pi/\partial Q = 0$ yields the familiar price = marginal cost requirement, and the second order condition for a maximum is $\partial^2\Pi/\partial Q^2 < 0$, that is, $\partial^2 TC/\partial Q^2 > 0$. Having obtained the profit-maximising level of Q from the first-order condition, the input levels then follow from the preceding cost-minimising input functions; substituting the optimal value of Q in terms of p, r, and w into these functions gives the derived demand functions for K and L - functions only of prices.

Alternatively, the profit-maximising values of Q, K, and L can be obtained in a single calculation by maximising

$$\Pi = pQ - rK - wL$$

subject to $Q = F(K,L)$. The Lagrangean is

$$\mathcal{L} = pQ - rK - wL - \lambda\{Q - F(K,L)\}$$

and the first-order conditions are

$$\frac{\partial \mathcal{L}}{\partial Q} = p - \lambda = 0$$

$$\frac{\partial \mathcal{L}}{\partial K} = -r + \lambda F_K = 0 \qquad \text{hence } r = pF_K,$$

$$\frac{\partial \mathcal{L}}{\partial L} = -w + \lambda F_L = 0 \qquad \text{hence } w = pF_L.$$

The two equations on the right are the <u>marginal productivity conditions</u>: for each input the value of its marginal product must equal its price, and solving these together with $Q = F(K,L)$ yields the profit-maximising levels of Q, K, and L.

Example

In the Cobb-Douglas case the marginal productivity conditions are

$$r = p\frac{\alpha Q}{K} \qquad \text{and} \qquad w = p\frac{\beta Q}{L},$$

thus $\alpha = \frac{rK}{pQ}$ and $\beta = \frac{wL}{pQ}$ can be interpreted as the respective shares of capital and labour in total output. The firm's optimal output and input levels result from solving these two equations together with $Q = AK^{\alpha}L^{\beta}$. Writing in logarithmic form, these are

$$\log Q = \log A + \alpha \log K + \beta \log L$$
$$\log Q + \log \alpha = \log K + \log \frac{r}{p}$$
$$\log Q + \log \beta = \log L + \log \frac{w}{p}$$

or, rearranging,

$$\begin{pmatrix} 1 & -\alpha & -\beta \\ 1 & -1 & 0 \\ 1 & 0 & -1 \end{pmatrix} \begin{pmatrix} \log Q \\ \log K \\ \log L \end{pmatrix} = \begin{pmatrix} \log A \\ \log \frac{r}{p} - \log \alpha \\ \log \frac{w}{p} - \log \beta \end{pmatrix}.$$

Can we solve for $\log Q$, $\log K$, and $\log L$, that is, can we obtain the reduced form? The system is of the correct order: there are as many equations as endogenous variables. But the determinant of the coefficient matrix is $1-\alpha-\beta$. So if $\alpha+\beta=1$ the matrix is singular and there is no solution: output is indeterminate in the constant returns case.

What has gone wrong? Cramer (1969, pp. 228-9) presents a verbal argument that in order for the marginal productivity conditions to have a determinate solution (for non-negative K and L) corresponding to maximum Π, there must be decreasing returns to scale. If prices are fixed, equal proportionate increases in K and L away from the optimum must, in order to yield smaller Π lead to a less than proportionate increase in Q. This argument is confirmed by examination of the second-order condition. The condition for maximum profit stated above is $\partial^2 TC/\partial Q^2 > 0$, and on differentiating our cost function twice we obtain

$$\frac{\partial^2 TC}{\partial Q^2} = k\,\frac{1}{n}\left(\frac{1}{n} - 1\right) Q^{-2+1/n}\, r^{\alpha/n}\, w^{\beta/n} .$$

Thus if $n=1$, $\partial^2 TC/\partial Q^2 = 0$ and the second order condition gives neither a maximum nor a minimum: marginal cost is constant (and equal to average cost). The condition boils down to $\frac{1}{n} - 1 > 0$, i.e. $n < 1$, and decreasing returns are required.

Alternatively, tackling the profit maximisation problem directly as on p. 34 and eliminating the constraint by substitution, we wish to maximise $\Pi = pF(K,L) - rK - wL$ with respect to K and L. Since the second and third terms are linear in K and L, the second-order conditions on Π are equivalent to those on the first term on the right hand side only. The requirement for a maximum is that the principal minors of the (Hessian) matrix of second order derivatives alternative in sign. This provides three conditions

$$F_{KK} < 0, \quad F_{LL} < 0 \quad \text{and} \quad F_{KK}.F_{LL} - (F_{KL})^2 > 0,$$

and for the Cobb-Douglas case you can check that the third condition provides the crucial requirement that $\alpha+\beta < 1$. The second order conditions therefore confirm Cramer's argument. Constant or increasing returns are incompatible with a determinate solution in this particular model of profit maximisation under perfect competition.

Two observations can be made about this conclusion. First, constant or increasing returns presumably cannot be ruled out as technical characteristics of the production function, certainly not before doing any estimation. Second, indeterminacy of Q, L and K in situations other than decreasing returns is unreasonable. They are in practice determined. So we have to reject the perfectly competitive hypothesis, where all prices are given and Q, K and L can be varied at will, if we wish to admit constant or increasing returns. One can do so by relaxing the infinite elasticity of demand assumption and add demand-for-product and supply-of-factor functions. The second order conditions of this somewhat more extensive system admit the possibility that $\alpha+\beta$ need not be less than 1 for an optimum. This line of argument however has not had much impact on empirical work.

The statistical model

Further difficulties emerge when we formulate appropriate statistical models for testing. We consider cross-section studies first. The parameters α and β are assumed equal for all firms, as are the prices which they face. Disturbance terms are added to account for variations in the data. This is done multiplicatively

$$Q_i = AK_i^{\alpha}L_i^{\beta}u_{1i}$$

to conform to the Cobb-Douglas representation and facilitate log taking. Thus u_{1i} is a positive factor taking values on either side of 1.

How can we interpret this disturbance term? Most often u_{1i} is held to represent the <u>technical or productive efficiency</u> of the ith entrepreneur - his knowledge, luck, skill, locational advantages, effort, and so forth. In effect the entrepreneur has the capacity to vary the multiplicative factor Au_i and so to change the position of a particular isoquant in achieving the optimum output from his inputs. (Note that if we considered a cross-section over time (panel data) then some of these factors might be particular to an entrepreneur for all time, without changing from one period to the next, while other factors affect all firms at a given point in time. This would introduce an error-components model, which disaggregates u_{it}, the disturbance term for the ith firm in year t, into a number of effects. If v_i is the effect of the constant entrepreneurial capacity of the ith firm, w_t embraces once-and-for-all effects on all firms (e.g. weather or industry-wide strikes) and ε_{it} is a pure random effect, then

$$u_{it} = v_i + w_t + \varepsilon_{it} .)$$

Random error terms are also introduced into the equations for the marginal productivity conditions:

$$\alpha \frac{Q_i}{K_i} = \frac{r}{p} u_{2i} , \qquad \beta \frac{Q_i}{L_i} = \frac{w}{p} u_{3i} .$$

These error terms are usually taken to reflect a firm's <u>economic or commercial efficiency</u>, its success in achieving its optimum position. Any departure from $u_{2i} = u_{3i} = 1$ implies failure to achieve profit maximization.

Linearising the system, we now have

$$\begin{aligned}
\log Q_i - \alpha \log K_i - \beta \log L_i &= \log A + \log u_{1i} \\
\log Q_i - \log K_i &= \log \frac{r}{p} - \log \alpha + \log u_{2i} \\
\log Q_i - \log L_i &= \log \frac{w}{p} - \log \beta + \log u_{3i}
\end{aligned}$$

Notice that even when $\alpha + \beta \neq 1$, so that the matrix $\mathbf{B}$ is non-singular, the production function is <u>not</u> identified. This follows from the rank and order conditions. Data could not distinguish the production function from some linear combination of the other two equations (remember that w, p, and r are constants). This becomes clear if we consider what would happen if we deflated our data for size of firm so that each firm had the same production function, with the same prices. In that case they would all be at the same point (ignoring random variation) on the same isoquant, and a line cannot be estimated from a single point. A number of approaches to this problem have been suggested.

From the order condition we know that identification can be achieved by adding exogenous variables to one of the other equations, and asserting that the variables do not appear in the production function. Consider the marginal productivity of capital condition. Including the stock of capital at the beginning of the period using partial-adjustment-type considerations seems reasonable, since investment does not occur instantaneously. However this suggestion takes us beyond the cross-section framework and raises time series problems. Alternatively the constant price assumption can be dropped. This can be done by, say, allowing wages or other input prices to vary regionally. More systematically we might abandon our assumptions of perfectly elastic input supply and output demand, with some prices becoming endogenous variables in an imperfectly competitive world. Identification of the production function can also be achieved if technical efficiency is not correlated with economic efficiency. If the error terms are independent then a linear combination of the production function and the marginal productivity conditions could not be mistaken for the production function, for it would have an error term which contains u_2 and u_3 and so is not independent of them, contrary to the specification of independence for the production function itself.

It might be appropriate under certain conditions to treat Q as a predetermined variable - this is realistic in the case of public utilities. The study of railroad transportation by Klein (1953, pp. 226-236) is discussed by Cramer, and Nerlove's study of electricity supply is described below. These industries have to supply on demand a product which cannot be stocked, and output is no longer an endogenous variable from the firm's point of view.

Cross-section analysis: returns to scale in electricity supply

The cross-section study of public utility enterprises by Nerlove (1963) illustrates how the problem posed by the lack of identifiability of the Cobb-Douglas production function in the standard competitive model can be overcome in certain circumstances. Identifiability is achieved by making use of particular features of the electricity supply industry, and parameters are estimated by working through the reduced form. These features are as follows.

1. Power is supplied on demand and cannot be stored. Hence output (Q) is beyond the firm's control, and can be treated as an exogenous variable.
2. Rates (prices) are set by the utility commision so that p is predetermined. 1 and 2 together imply that total revenue is predetermined.
3. Labour is unionised with wage rates set by long-term contracts so that the individual firm is a price-taker in the short-run labour market. (In the long run it might be assumed that the contracts are in fact competitive, but this assumption is not required.)
4. Capital markets are assumed highly competitive.
5. Fuel contracts are long term and competitively priced so that the firm is again a price-taker in the short run.

Assumptions 3, 4 and 5 imply that factor prices are given to a particular firm, but they are not identical across the whole industry. Such variation in prices achieves identification of the production function in the model on p. 37, and permits the estimation of a cost function across firms. Adding assumptions 1 and 2 (pQ predetermined) implies that profit-maximization is equivalent to cost minimisation, so the analysis of p. 31 is relevant. Taking a Cobb-Douglas production function, the cost-minimising input functions derived on p. 32 are <u>reduced form</u> equations under these assumptions, and the cost function is simply a linear combination of these, giving endogenous total costs in terms of exogenous input prices and output. (Data on total costs were available to Nerlove.) The Cobb-Douglas production function is slightly generalised to the case of three inputs, as follows:

$$Q = Ax_1^{\alpha_1} x_2^{\alpha_2} x_3^{\alpha_3}$$

where x_1 is the amount of labour input, x_2 the amount of capital input, and x_3 the amount of fuel input (p_i, i=1,2,3 denoting their respective prices). A derivation as on p. 32 then leads to the generalised cost function

$$\log TC = \log k + \frac{1}{n}\log Q + \frac{\alpha_1}{n}\log p_1 + \frac{\alpha_2}{n}\log p_2 + \frac{\alpha_3}{n}\log p_3$$

where

$$n = \alpha_1 + \alpha_2 + \alpha_3$$

and

$$k = n(A\alpha_1^{\alpha_1}\alpha_2^{\alpha_2}\alpha_3^{\alpha_3})^{-1/n} \quad .$$

The four variables on the right hand side are all predetermined, and a direct estimate of the degree of returns to scale is possible. A slight problem is that the parameters are overidentified: the five coefficients (k, $1/n$, α_1/n, α_2/n, α_3/n) are functions of only four parameters (α_1, α_2, α_3, A). But $\alpha_1+\alpha_2+\alpha_3 = n$ and so the extra degree of freedom can be removed by imposing this restriction on the estimates. This can be done by dividing TC and two prices by the remaining price, say p_3, that is, by subtracting $\log p_3$ from both sides. In this way Nerlove's <u>Model A</u> is derived:

$$\log TC - \log p_3 = \log k + \frac{1}{n}\log Q + \frac{\alpha_1}{n}\log p_1 + \frac{\alpha_2}{n}\log p_2 + \left(\frac{\alpha_3}{n} - 1\right)\log p_3,$$

and as the restriction gives $\frac{\alpha_3}{n} - 1 = -\frac{\alpha_1}{n} - \frac{\alpha_2}{n}$ we have

$$\log\left(\frac{TC}{p_3}\right) = \log k + \frac{1}{n}\log Q + \frac{\alpha_1}{n}\log\frac{p_1}{p_3} + \frac{\alpha_2}{n}\log\frac{p_2}{p_3} \; .$$

There are now only four coefficients, from which unique estimates of the four parameters can be derived.

This form assumes that the sample data on the prices of inputs varies across firms. Suppose the price of capital (p_2) does not vary. In that case p_2 becomes part of the constant term and the overidentification does not arise. We have <u>Model B</u>:

$$\log TC = k' + \frac{1}{n}\log Q + \frac{\alpha_1}{n}\log p_1 + \frac{\alpha_3}{n}\log p_3$$

where

$$k' = \log k + \frac{\alpha_2}{n}\log p_2 \, .$$

There is no need to place a restriction on this equation, since there are four coefficients giving estimates of the four parameters, an estimate of α_2 being derived from the estimates of n, α_1, and α_3.

An error term of the multiplicative (technical efficiency) type added to the production function carries through to the cost function. We say that u has a "log-normal" distribution if log u is normally distributed, and we usually assume that log u has a zero mean. If this error term obeys the classical assumptions of independence and constant variance, then the resulting coefficient estimates are unbiased, efficient, and consistent. But the parameter estimates lose the unbiasedness property because in deriving them from the regression coefficients non-linear operations are involved. For example, to estimate n we take the reciprocal of the coefficient on the output variable and although that coefficient provides an unbiased estimate of $1/n$, its reciprocal does not provide an unbiased estimate of n, for $E(1/b) \neq 1/E(b)$. So the parameter estimates only remain consistent; they are in effect indirect least squares estimates (*IE*, §5.6).

Nerlove had a cross-section sample of 145 firms. Previous studies had been done at the plant level, finding $n \geq 1$, though some reduction in returns might be expected when a number of plants are combined into a single firm. Both Models A and B found $\hat{n} \simeq 1.39$ and had surprisingly high R^2 values for cross-section studies. However this masked a number of problems, in particular $\hat{\alpha}_2$ was not significantly different from zero (which may reflect either the lack of short-run variability of capital input or other data problems with the capital price variable).

The residuals were examined to check for any systematic influence of omitted variables. Plotting them against log Q revealed the situation illustrated in Figure 5. This suggests non-constant error

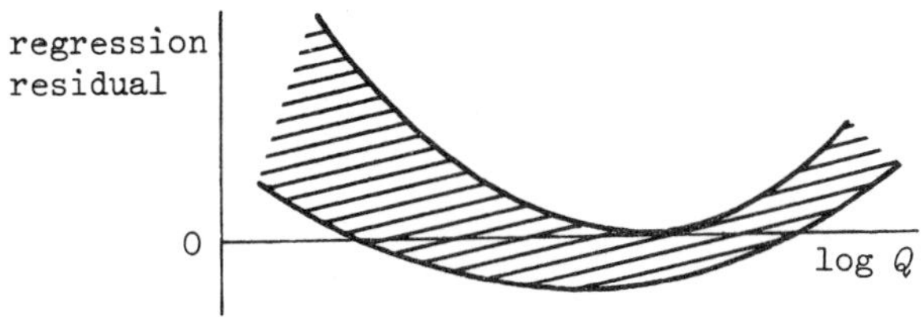

Figure 5

variance (heteroscedasticity), and a relation of residual variance to size (output of firm). This pattern is not surprising if in fact the relationship is not genuinely linear in the logarithms. As an illustration, consider the residuals obtained when a log-log relationship is fitted to data which obey a linear relationship, as shown in Figure 6. This is drawn with arithmetic scales on both axes, assuming

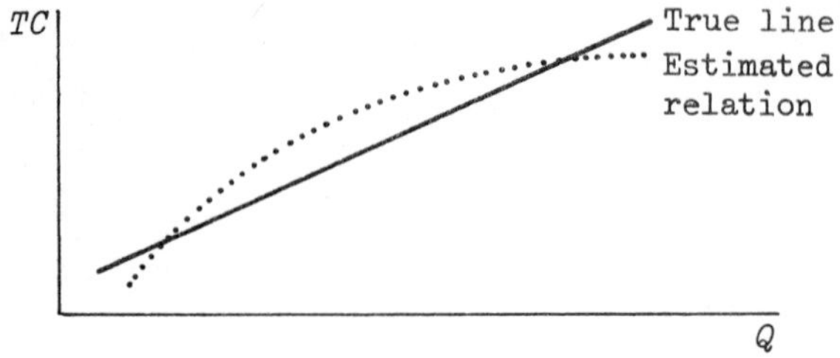

Figure 6

that the estimated log-log equation has a coefficient less than one. As the independent variable increases, the residuals first tend to be positive, then they are all negative, and finally again all positive, instead of showing random variability throughout. Nerlove also uses the Durbin-Watson statistic. Although this is normally associated with time series data and has no obvious cross-section interpretation in general, where there does exist a meaningful ordering of the data (to correspond to the chronological ordering of time series data) it can be used as a check for mis-specification. Here the data were ordered by size of firm, as measured by output, and the Durbin-Watson statistic indicated highly significant positive serial correlation. An economic explanation can be provided by setting up the traditional cost function, plotting TC against Q as in Figure 7, corresponding to

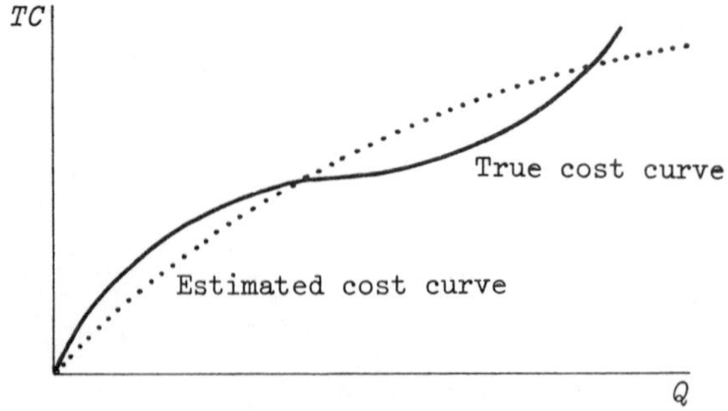

Figure 7

a U-shaped long-run average cost curve. In this case n is not constant and independent of Q but is inversely related to it, with increasing returns at small values of Q and decreasing returns at large values of Q. If the true TC function is of this type then fitting a log-log relationship would produce the pattern of residuals found by Nerlove, as it underestimates TC for small and large values of Q, and overestimates in the intermediate range.

Nerlove tackled this situation by splitting his sample of 145 firms into five groups of 29, ordered by output. He hoped in this way to approximate the continuous TC curve by a set of log-log segments. For each sub-group of firms, the total cost function was estimated, thus for each segment of the cost curve an estimate of the degree of returns to scale was obtained. Sure enough n decreased with size of firm - smallest firms: $\hat{n} \simeq 2\frac{1}{2}$; medium firms: $\hat{n} \simeq 1\frac{1}{2}$; largest firms: n not significantly different from 1. A test of the results is provided by comparing the residual sum of squares over the five segments with the original residual sum of squares obtained when a single relationship is assumed to hold over the whole range of output. The reduction in the residual sum of squares by stratifying the data into the five sub-groups was indeed significant. Nevertheless a problem which remained was the erratic elasticity estimates in the various segments. Nerlove's attempt to surmount this problem involved restricting the price variables in different groups to have the same coefficient and allowing only the coefficient of log Q to vary. This is equivalent to imposing "neutral variations", in that marginal rates of substitution are not affected. (m.r.s. of x_i for x_j = $\frac{\partial Q/\partial x_j}{\partial Q/\partial x_i} = \frac{\alpha_j}{\alpha_i}\frac{x_i}{x_j}$. Allowing the coefficients α_i/n to vary between groups means that not only the α's but also the m.r.s. varies, whereas constraining these to be the same in all groups while $1/n$ differs between groups keeps the m.r.s. constant, for the α's vary in proportion to n.) This approach, however, seemed not to work on statistical tests, and hence the neutral variation hypothesis is rejected.

The two strong conclusions are (i) that there are variations in n with size of firm and (ii) that there are increasing returns to scale at the firm level. In addition to illustrating the derivation

D

and estimation of a reduced form equation under specific institutional conditions, Nerlove's study provides a good example of the value of examining residuals to test the appropriateness of a model.

Estimation from factor shares

Remaining within the cross-section context, we can examine Klein's alternative to the reduced form estimation adopted by Nerlove. This involves working from a structural equation which is identified.

We noted that in a model comprising a Cobb-Douglas production function and two marginal productivity conditions derived from profit-maximisation under perfect competition, the production function was not identified (p.37). But the marginal productivity conditions are identified by the standard conditions - each excludes one variable of the model (prices are constant, remember) and has one homogeneous linear restriction on its coefficients. Taking the labour marginal productivity condition as an example, the equation was obtained from the requirement

$$\beta \frac{Q_i}{L_i} = \frac{w}{p} u_{3i} \qquad i = 1,\ldots,N.$$

This can alternatively be written

$$\log \beta = \log \left(\frac{wL_i}{pQ_i}\right) + \log u_{3i},$$

and given N observations we can then estimate $\log \beta$ as an average:

$$\widehat{\log \beta} = \frac{1}{N} \sum_{i=1}^{N} \log \left(\frac{wL_i}{pQ_i}\right).$$

What are the properties of this estimator ? It is unbiased and consistent if $E(\log u_{3i}) = 0$. Relationships between the endogenous variables Q_i and L_i and the disturbance term u_{3i} do not cause any difficulty in evaluating $E(\widehat{\log \beta})$ for u_3 enters additively - the expected value of a sum of variables is the sum of the expected values of the variables whether or not they are independent. The unbiasedness property disappears but consistency remains when we unscramble an estimate of β, as antilog $(\widehat{\log \beta})$ or $e^{\widehat{\log \beta}}$. The resulting estimate is the sample geometric mean of labour's share in total output:

$$\hat{\beta} = \sqrt[N]{\prod_{i=1}^{N} \frac{wL_i}{pQ_i}} \,.$$

The assumption here is that the marginal product is being equated to the wage rate so these estimates cannot be used to study that question - it is a maintained hypothesis. However the two estimates $\hat{\alpha}$ and $\hat{\beta}$ will tend to have a sum close to 1 if the standard accounting convention of assuming all revenue is distributed to capital or labour has been followed. That is, the data obey $pQ = rK + wL$. In that case a calculated arithmetic-mean factor shares estimate has $\tilde{\alpha} + \tilde{\beta} = 1$. (Variations in prices might give slight departures from 1). The above geometric mean estimate will almost obey this if the accounting convention has been observed - the use of geometric means will cause the two estimates, $\hat{\alpha}$ and $\hat{\beta}$, to have a sum slightly less than 1, (Walters (1963, p.21) per contra). So the use of such an accounting identity to calculate the quantity of capital input, for example, presents a fresh identification problem. Much was made of the correspondence between the least squares regression coefficients and estimated factor shares in some of the early time series studies to which we now turn.

Time series studies

How did the early time series studies apparently turn out so well, given all the above-mentioned difficulties in specifying a suitable model to enable a Cobb-Douglas production function to be identified? Cramer uses numerical results from a later study by Douglas (1948) to illustrate the earlier Cobb-Douglas (1928) approach. Given aggregate time series data on the three volume variables (Q_t, L_t, K_t), least squares estimates are calculated for the equation

$$\log Q_t = \log A + \alpha \log K_t + \beta \log L_t + u_t \,.$$

Typically $\hat{\alpha} + \hat{\beta} \simeq 1$, for example with U.S. data for all manufacturing industry, 1899-1922, $\hat{\alpha} = 0.25$ (s.e. 0.05) and $\hat{\beta} = 0.73$ (0.12). So constant returns to scale are imposed and the equation

$$\log \left(\frac{Q_t}{K_t}\right) = \log A + \beta \log \left(\frac{L_t}{K_t}\right) + u_t$$

estimated, giving $\hat{\beta} = 0.76$ (0.04). Note the decrease in the standard error - one explanation may be that multicollinearity between $\log K_t$ and $\log L_t$ in the former version has been avoided by the transformation, so increasing the accuracy of the estimate. (If multicollinearity was originally present we would expect less precise estimates with somewhat inflated standard errors.) Under perfect competition (and omitting the error term) the marginal productivity condition gives $\beta = \frac{wL}{pQ}$, and the average labour share for the years 1909-1918 is calculated as 0.74. This correspondence apparently verifies marginal productivity theory as well as the Cobb-Douglas function. But wait!

Suppose again the accounting convention $p_t Q_t = r_t K_t + w_t L_t$ holds in all periods, so that

$$Q_t = \left(\frac{r_t}{p_t}\right) K_t + \left(\frac{w_t}{p_t}\right) L_t .$$

Assume also that the price ratios $(\frac{r}{p}, \frac{w}{p})$ are constant for all t, so that

$$Q_t = \left(\frac{r}{p}\right) K_t + \left(\frac{w}{p}\right) L_t .$$

(Cramer (1969, pp.236-7) overstates the requirement for the following derivation. We do not require constant prices, only constant price ratios, which is more likely if prices move in step.) It can then be shown that the equation as estimated by Douglas and his co-workers is a close approximation to this identity in the data and there is very little point in attempting to rediscover it. If all revenue is paid to either capital or labour it is difficult to distinguish between this accounting identity and the estimated equation. To see this correspondence we need a linear approximation to the estimated equation. Recall that the least squares regression line

$$\log Q_t = \log A + \alpha \log K_t + \beta \log L_t + u_t$$

will pass through the point of sample means:

$$\overline{\log Q} = \log A + \alpha\, \overline{\log K} + \beta\, \overline{\log L} + \bar{u}.$$

Now let $\bar{Q}$, $\bar{K}$, $\bar{L}$ be antilogs of $\overline{\log Q}$ etc (geometric means). Subtracting these two equations, so that the constant term vanishes, and remembering that $\log Q_t - \log \bar{Q} = \log (Q_t/\bar{Q})$ etc. gives

$$\log \left(\frac{Q_t}{\bar{Q}}\right) = \alpha \log \left(\frac{K_t}{\bar{K}}\right) + \beta \log \left(\frac{L_t}{\bar{L}}\right) + u_t - \bar{u}.$$

Now

$$\log \left(\frac{Q_t}{\bar{Q}}\right) = \log \left(\frac{\bar{Q}+Q_t-\bar{Q}}{\bar{Q}}\right) = \log \left(1 + \frac{Q_t-\bar{Q}}{\bar{Q}}\right)$$

and

$$\log (1+x) = x - \frac{1}{2}x^2 + \frac{1}{3}x^3 - \ldots, \quad -1 < x < 1.$$

Here it is certain that $(Q_t-\bar{Q})/\bar{Q} < 1$, and it is probably close to zero For x small we can approximate $\log (1+x)$ by x, using only the first term of the power series and neglecting terms in x^2, x^3,... which will be very small. So

$$\log \left(1 + \frac{Q_t-\bar{Q}}{\bar{Q}}\right) \simeq \frac{Q_t-\bar{Q}}{\bar{Q}} = \frac{Q_t}{\bar{Q}} - 1,$$

and we can approximate the estimated log-linear relationship by

$$\frac{Q_t}{\bar{Q}} - 1 \simeq a\left(\frac{K_t}{\bar{K}} - 1\right) + b\left(\frac{L_t}{\bar{L}} - 1\right)$$

or

$$Q_t \simeq a\,\frac{\bar{Q}}{\bar{K}}\,K_t + b\,\frac{\bar{Q}}{\bar{K}}\,L_t + (1-a-b)\,\bar{Q}.$$

Since, if price ratios are constant, the data also satisfy

$$Q_t = (\frac{r}{p}) K_t + (\frac{w}{p}) L_t$$

we expect

$$\frac{r}{p} \simeq a \frac{\overline{Q}}{\overline{K}}, \qquad \frac{w}{p} \simeq b \frac{\overline{Q}}{\overline{L}}, \qquad 1 - a - b \simeq 0.$$

Thus the estimated coefficients, a and b, correspond closely to factor shares, $a \simeq r\overline{K}/p\overline{Q}$, $b \simeq w\overline{L}/p\overline{Q}$, and exhibit constant returns to scale, since the estimating equation cannot be distinguished from the accounting identity. So perhaps these Cobb-Douglas results and the apparent support for constant returns are not as strong as was first supposed.

Technical change

Estimation of a production function with a fixed constant term rules out one of the simplest ways in which the influence of technical change can be incorporated. The problem in time series studies of technical change is to distinguish movements along a production function from shifts of the function, assumed due to technical progress. We consider disembodied technical progress, which arrives as "manna from heaven" with benefits freely available. The resulting shifts of the production function are represented by including a time variable:

$$Q = F(K, L, t).$$

To benefit from technical progress embodied in capital or labour the firm must invest in new capital goods or labour. Advances are embodied in capital goods of different vintages, thus capital is no longer assumed homogeneous - new machines are more productive than old machines.

A neutral disembodied technical change (in Hicks' definition) is one which neither saves nor uses either factor, and so leaves the marginal rate of substitution unaltered. For a given factor-price ratio technical change shifts the isoquants inwards. Hicks-neutral technical change leaves the slope of the isoquants along a ray through the origin unchanged: there is no incentive to vary factor proportions unless relative factor prices change. If on the other hand the production function shifts so that (say) the marginal product of capital rises relative to that of labour for each K-L combination - i.e. the marginal rate of substitution of K for L falls - then technical change is capital-using (labour-saving) and non-neutral.

In the Cobb-Douglas case the easiest way to incorporate neutral technical progress is to allow the scale parameter A to vary, for this will not affect the marginal rate of substitution:

$$Q_t = A(t)K_t^{\alpha}L_t^{\beta}.$$

An early attempt by Tinbergen in this framework used the form $A(t) = A_0e^{\lambda t}$, which is equivalent to introducing a trend term into the log-linear regression, but the problems of identification remain. The only way to obtain non-neutral change with the Cobb-Douglas function is to allow the ratio $\frac{\alpha}{\beta}$ to vary: if α rises relative to β then technical change is capital-using, and vice versa. Variation in the elasticity of substitution would also result in non-neutral technical change, but the Cobb-Douglas function has a constant elasticity of one.

Solow (1957) sidesteps the identification problem in the context of constant returns by abandoning the Cobb-Douglas specification and making use of marginal productivity conditions in an attempt to differentiate shifts of from movements along the production function. Assuming that technical progress is neutral and disembodied (an untested hypothesis in Solow's work), we have

$$Q_t = A(t)\ F(K_t, L_t).$$

Differentiating with respect to time and denoting the derivatives by putting a dot over the variable, hence $\frac{dQ}{dt} = \dot{Q}$, we have

$$\dot{Q} = \dot{A}\ F(K_t, L_t) + A\frac{\partial F}{\partial K}\dot{K} + A\frac{\partial F}{\partial L}\dot{L}.$$

Dividing by Q gives an equation for the proportionate rate of change of output:

$$\frac{\dot{Q}}{Q} = \frac{\dot{A}F(K_t,L_t)}{Q} + A\frac{\partial F}{\partial K}\frac{\dot{K}}{Q} + A\frac{\partial F}{\partial L}\frac{\dot{L}}{Q}.$$

Now we add the assumption that factors are paid their marginal products, $\frac{\partial Q}{\partial K} = \frac{r}{p}$ and $\frac{\partial Q}{\partial L} = \frac{w}{p}$. In Solow's notation the shares of capital and labour are denoted respectively by $w_K = rK/pQ$ and $w_L = wL/pQ$, thus with the above assumption we have

$$w_K = \frac{\partial Q}{\partial K}\frac{K}{Q} = A\frac{\partial F}{\partial K}\frac{K}{Q}, \qquad w_L = \frac{\partial Q}{\partial L}\frac{L}{Q} = A\frac{\partial F}{\partial L}\frac{L}{Q},$$

and the preceding equation becomes

$$\frac{\dot{Q}}{Q} = \frac{\dot{A}}{A} + w_K\frac{\dot{K}}{K} + w_L\frac{\dot{L}}{L}.$$

Assuming constant returns to scale gives $w_L + w_K = 1$ by Euler's theorem, and we can convert to per capita variables. Let $q = \frac{Q}{L}$ and $k = \frac{K}{L}$. The proportionate rates of change of the per capita variables are expressed in terms of the proportionate rates of change of the total volume variables as follows:

$$\dot{q} = \frac{\dot{Q}}{L} - \frac{Q}{L^2}\dot{L}, \text{ and so } \frac{\dot{q}}{q} = \frac{\dot{Q}}{Q} - \frac{\dot{L}}{L};$$

also

$$\frac{\dot{k}}{k} = \frac{\dot{K}}{K} - \frac{\dot{L}}{L}.$$

Substituting in, we have

$$\frac{\dot{q}}{q} + \frac{\dot{L}}{L} = \frac{\dot{A}}{A} + w_K\left(\frac{\dot{k}}{k} + \frac{\dot{L}}{L}\right) + w_L\frac{\dot{L}}{L}$$

and since $w_K + w_L = 1$ this becomes

$$\frac{\dot{q}}{q} = \frac{\dot{A}}{A} + w_K \frac{\dot{k}}{k}.$$

Using this relation and annual data on output per man-hour, capital per man-hour, and the share of capital, the technical change index $\dot{A}/A$ can be estimated year by year. Approximating $\frac{\dot{q}}{q}$ by $\frac{\Delta q}{q}$ (first differences in annual data) the time series of $\frac{\Delta A}{A}$ is then constructed. (Solow uses a forward difference: $\Delta A(t) = A(t+1) - A(t)$, but this is of no consequence.) Having calculated the changes $\Delta A(t)/A(t)$, and assuming an arbitrary starting value $A(1) = 1$, a series for $A(t)$ can be constructed recursively:

$$A(t+1) = A(t) \left(1 + \frac{\Delta A(t)}{A(t)}\right).$$

The resulting series has a strong upward trend; the average rate of technical progress in the U.S. over the period 1909 - 1949 was 1.5% per annum.

Having got an estimate of how much the production function was shifting, Solow then asked how much of the increase in output per man-hour during the forty years was due to technical change (I in Figure 8), and how much was due to the increase in k (II). An idea

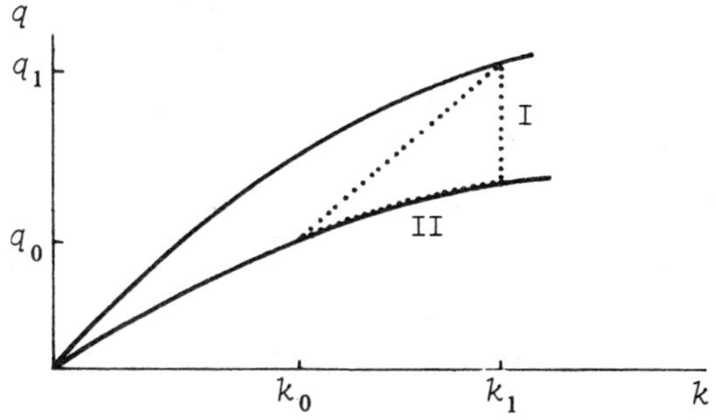

Figure 8

of the fixed function corrected for technical progress can be obtained by dividing $q(t)$ by $A(t)$. This estimates what would have occurred without technical change, that is the increase in output per man-hour attributable to the increase in capital. Solow found that technical change over the sample period accounted for 90% of the improvement in output per man-hour, and growth of capital the remaining 10%. As Solow acknowledged, his measure is a catch-all, incorporating any kind of shift in the production function - "slowdowns, speedups, improvements in the education of the labour force" (an embodied technical change) all appear as "technical change". A further difficulty with an aggregate measure such as this is that it ignores changes in the composition of output. For example if the economy utilizes more intensively sectors which enjoy comparative advantages, but there is no technical progress, nevertheless the overall productivity measure will increase.

When $\frac{q}{A}$ is plotted against the capital-labour ratio as an indication of the underlying production function corrected for technical change, the Cobb-Douglas form log $(\frac{q}{A})$ on log k does as well as anything else. This is not too surprising since the Cobb-Douglas function would fit perfectly if factor shares were constant, and in fact they show little variability. (Solow spent some time in his original paper attempting to explain the 1943-1949 observations, which did not lie on the general relation between q/A and k given by the other observations. It turns out that these were the result of a computational error; see, for example, Hogan (1958) or the footnote to this effect on p.330 of the Solow paper as reprinted in Mueller (1969).)

The CES production function

Neo-classical economics emphasises the substitutability between factors of production, the ease of which is measured by the elasticity parameter, σ. The Cobb-Douglas function constrains σ to equal one, which may or may not be a good approximation. The constant elasticity of substitution (CES) production function also constrains the value of σ to be constant, but not necessarily equal to 1. The elasticity of substitution is then constant in the sense that it does not change with changes in relative prices or factor inputs - its value is determined by the underlying technology and may change with technical progress.

In the Cobb-Douglas case, under competitive conditions, the labour marginal productivity equation can be written

$$\log (Q/L) = - \log \beta + \log (w/p),$$

and so output per head varies with the real wage rate (logarithmically) with a coefficient of unity. In contrast, Arrow, Chenery, Minhas, and Solow (1961) - referred to as SMAC - observed cross-section regressions with a coefficient not equal to one,

$$\log (Q/L) = a + b \log (w/p),$$

and derived the CES production function as a solution to this equation. The function is

$$Q = \gamma\{\delta K^{-\rho} + (1-\delta)L^{-\rho}\}^{-\nu/\rho} .$$

Writing the right hand side as $F(K,L)$, then $F(hK,hL) = h^{\nu}F(K,L)$ and ν gives the degree of homogeneity: in the original SMAC study ν was taken equal to one and so constant returns were imposed, although the independent derivation by Brown and de Cani (1963) permits any degree of returns to scale. γ is a scale parameter which can be used to denote efficiency: a shift in γ is an example of neutral technical change. δ indicates the degree to which technology is capital intensive, and when the production function is embedded in a particular economic model δ can be interpreted as the distribution parameter. ρ is the substitution parameter equal to $(1-\sigma)/\sigma$ as we shall see. Rewriting the production function as

$$Q^{-\rho/\nu} = \gamma^{-\rho/\nu}\{\delta K^{-\rho} + (1-\delta)L^{-\rho}\}$$

and differentiating with respect to K and L we have

$$-\frac{\rho}{\nu} Q^{-1-\rho/\nu} \frac{\partial Q}{\partial K} = -\rho\gamma^{-\rho/\nu} \delta K^{-\rho-1}$$

and

$$-\frac{\rho}{\nu} Q^{-1-\rho/\nu} \frac{\partial Q}{\partial L} = -\rho\gamma^{-\rho/\nu} (1-\delta)L^{-\rho-1}$$

therefore

$$\frac{\partial Q}{\partial K} = \nu\delta\gamma^{-\rho/\nu} \frac{Q^{1+\rho/\nu}}{K^{1+\rho}} , \qquad \frac{\partial Q}{\partial L} = \nu(1-\delta)\gamma^{-\rho/\nu} \frac{Q^{1+\rho/\nu}}{L^{1+\rho}} .$$

Thus the marginal rate of substitution is

$$R = \frac{\partial Q}{\partial L}/\frac{\partial Q}{\partial K} = \frac{1 - \delta}{\delta} (\frac{K}{L})^{1+\rho} .$$

Taking logs:

$$\log R = \log (\frac{1-\delta}{\delta}) + (1+\rho) \log (\frac{K}{L})$$

and so

$$\sigma = \frac{d \log (K/L)}{d \log R} = \frac{1}{1+\rho} .$$

(It can be shown that the CES production function reduces to the Cobb-Douglas as $\sigma \to 1$, i.e. as $\rho \to 0$.)

A major problem with the CES production function is that unlike the Cobb-Douglas, we cannot transform it into a linear-in-parameters form by operations such as taking logarithms. There is no method of linearising that will sort out the parameters and variables to give a directly estimable exact representation. Linear approximations have been used, alternatively estimation has proceeded via side relations such as marginal productivity conditions and labour's share which result from adding standard economic assumptions to the CES specification. Nor is the cost function much help in this case. Following the general procedure described on p.31 we have

$$\frac{F_L}{F_K} = \frac{1-\delta}{\delta} (\frac{K}{L})^{1+\rho} = \frac{w}{r},$$

thus

$$L = K\left(\frac{1-\delta}{\delta}\frac{r}{w}\right)^{\sigma}.$$

The production function can be written

$$\left(\frac{Q}{\gamma}\right)^{-\rho/\nu} = \delta K^{-\rho} + (1-\delta)L^{-\rho}$$

$$= K^{-\rho}\{\delta + (1-\delta)^{\sigma}\delta^{\rho\sigma}\left(\frac{r}{w}\right)^{-\rho\sigma}\},$$

so the cost-minimising level of capital input is

$$K = \left(\frac{Q}{\gamma}\right)^{1/\nu}\{\delta + (1-\delta)^{\sigma}\,\delta^{\rho\sigma}\left(\frac{r}{w}\right)^{-\rho\sigma}\}^{1/\rho}$$

$$= \left(\frac{Q}{\gamma}\right)^{1/\nu} r^{-\sigma}\,\delta^{\sigma}\{\delta^{\sigma} r^{1-\sigma} + (1-\delta)^{\sigma} w^{1-\sigma}\}^{1/\rho}. \qquad (\rho\sigma+\sigma=1)$$

Similarly for labour input we obtain

$$L = \left(\frac{Q}{\gamma}\right)^{1/\nu} w^{-\sigma}(1-\delta)^{\sigma}\{\delta^{\sigma} r^{1-\sigma} + (1-\delta)^{\sigma} w^{1-\sigma}\}^{1/\rho},$$

hence the cost function is

$$TC = rK + wL$$

$$= \left(\frac{Q}{\gamma}\right)^{1/\nu}\{\delta^{\sigma} r^{1-\sigma} + (1-\delta)^{\sigma} w^{1-\sigma}\}^{1/1-\sigma}. \qquad \left(1+\frac{1}{\rho}=\frac{1}{1-\sigma}\right)$$

(Note that there are small slips in the CES cost functions given by both Nerlove (1967, p.113) and Walters (1963, p.7).) Again this cannot be expressed in a linear-in-parameters fashion, and so even in the economic context in which Nerlove estimated a Cobb-Douglas cost function, direct estimation of the CES parameters is not possible: it is necessary to follow less direct routes.

Estimation of the CES function

Using our economic model in the usual way we have the marginal productivity conditions $\partial Q/\partial K = r/p$ and $\partial Q/\partial L = w/p$. In the constant returns case (ν=1), the second condition gives

$$(1-\delta)\gamma^{-\rho}\left(\frac{Q}{L}\right)^{1+\rho} = \frac{w}{p}\,.$$

Thus

$$(1-\delta)\gamma^{-\rho} = \frac{w}{p}\left(\frac{L}{Q}\right)^{1+\rho} \quad \text{or} \quad \{(1-\delta)\gamma^{-\rho}\}^{1/1+\rho} = \left(\frac{wL}{pQ}\right)\left(\frac{w}{p}\right)^{\sigma-1}$$

and

$$\log\left(\frac{wL}{pQ}\right) = \sigma \log(1-\delta) + (1-\sigma)\log\left(\frac{w}{p}\right) + (\sigma-1)\log\gamma.$$

If σ=1 as in the Cobb-Douglas case, then labour's share is independent of both the wage rate and neutral technical progress. If $\sigma < 1$, labour's share rises if wages increase faster than technical progress. Using this as a time series equation let neutral technical progress occur via changes in the parameter γ, i.e. $\gamma_t = \gamma_0 e^{\lambda t}$, where λ is some constant rate. Then $\log\gamma_t = \log\gamma_0 + \lambda t$ and

$$\log\left(\frac{wL}{pQ}\right)_t = \{\sigma\log(1-\delta) + (\sigma-1)\log\gamma_0\} + (1-\sigma)\log\left(\frac{w}{p}\right)_t + (\sigma-1)\lambda t$$

so a trend variable appears in the share of labour relation. This was used by SMAC to reestimate Solow's time series technical progress data, with the follow results:

$$(1-\hat{\sigma}) = 0.431, \quad (\hat{\sigma}-1)\hat{\lambda} = -.003,$$

hence

$$\hat{\sigma} = 0.569, \quad \hat{\lambda} = 0.008.$$

This provides evidence against the hypothesis that σ=1, and provides an estimate of technical progress equivalent to a rate of 1.8% per annum.

In their cross-section study, not having data on capital or rate of return, SMAC estimated a further side relation derived from the labour marginal productivity condition.

$$\frac{Q}{L} = \{(1-\delta)\gamma^{-\rho}\}^{-1/1+\rho} \quad (\frac{w}{p})^{1/1+\rho} \;,$$

and

$$\log\ (Q/L) = -\sigma\ \log\{(1-\delta)\gamma^{-\rho}\} + \sigma\ \log\ (w/p),$$

so a 1% increase in real wages is associated with a σ% increase in average labour productivity. In fact this was the first SMAC regression equation referred to above (p. 53), and we now see that b, the coefficient of log (w/p), provides an estimate of σ. The equation was estimated for each of 24 industries from a cross-section of up to 19 countries. Of the 24 values of $\hat{\sigma}$ all but one were less than 1 (and the exceptional value of 1.011 was not significantly different from 1). Ten were significantly different from 1 at the 5% level or better and four more at the 10% level. It was therefore claimed that $\sigma \neq 1$ and the CES function should be preferred to the Cobb-Douglas.

However, suppose that there are non-constant returns so that the labour marginal productivity condition becomes

$$\frac{\partial Q}{\partial L} = \nu(1-\delta)\gamma^{-\rho/\nu}(\frac{Q}{L})^{1+\rho}Q^{-\rho+\rho/\nu} = \frac{w}{p}.$$

The regression equation is then

$$\log\ (\frac{Q}{L}) = \text{constant} + \sigma\ \log\ (\frac{w}{p}) + \rho\sigma(1 - \frac{1}{\nu})\ \log\ Q$$

There is no estimation of returns to scale in the original SMAC paper; $\nu = 1$ is assumed, equivalent to setting the last coefficient in this regression equal to zero. That is, log Q only appears on the right hand side if $\nu \neq 1$, and perhaps that possibility should be investigated.

The main problem with the SMAC study lies in the sample data collected for these nineteen countries. The unweighted across-industry average wage (1954) ranged from \$3,841 in the U.S. to \$213 in Iraq! Fuchs(1963) therefore divided the countries into two groups - more and less developed - and estimated for each separately. Again assuming constant returns he showed that the intercept term differed significantly between the two groups but the slope coefficient did not. In all but three of the 24 cases the estimated elasticity of substitution was greater than that obtained by SMAC, and it was significantly different from one in only two cases. However, the intercept term was smaller for the more developed countries, whereas one might expect it to be greater on the grounds that the more developed countries either are more efficient - they have a higher value-added per head for a given wage rate, that is, a higher value of γ - or employ a more capital-intensive technology and have a higher value of δ. Fuchs explained this by the suggestion that observed wages in less developed economies fail to reflect labour costs fully. His argument is illustrated in Figure 9.

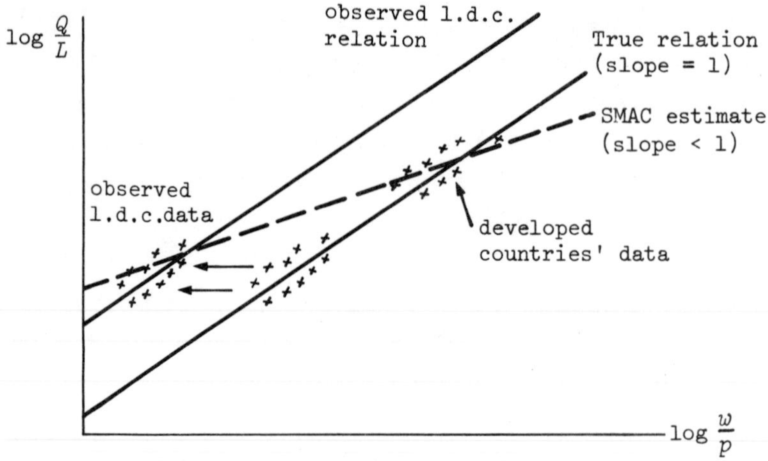

Figure 9

The true relationship lies along a line with a slope of 1. But the under-recording of labour costs in less developed countries shifts observations on them to the left. The less developed countries will then be found to have a higher intercept term, but the slopes for developed and less developed will be the same. The SMAC estimate was based on data for both types of economy and so has a lower slope and higher intercept than the true (presumably Cobb-Douglas) relationship.

An alternative argument which gets to the same result is that the left-hand solid line is the "true" relation and the developed countries' observations are shifted to the right by virtue of trade union pressure, which achieves a higher real wage for given productivity than would be the case in less developed countries with less trade union activity.

A further example of a side relation permitting the estimation of certain CES parameters is provided by equating the marginal rate of substitution to the factor price ratio:

$$\frac{F_L}{F_K} = \frac{1-\delta}{\delta} \left(\frac{K}{L}\right)^{1+\rho} = \frac{w}{r},$$

then

$$\log \left(\frac{K}{L}\right) = \sigma \log \left(\frac{\delta}{1-\delta}\right) + \sigma \log \left(\frac{w}{r}\right).$$

Given data on $\frac{K}{L}$ and relative prices, say time series data for a particular firm subject to changing demand, or cross-section data as in Nerlove's electricity supply study, from this regression estimates of two CES parameters can be derived: $\hat{\rho}$ follows from the estimate of σ and $\hat{\delta}$ from the estimated constant term. Note that δ is not invariant to units of measurement (though σ is) and so cannot be readily compared between different studies. It can be standardised by using relative changes of variables or by converting data to index number form. The latter procedure has the advantage of also standardising the $\frac{K}{L}$ ratio.

The disturbance term enters this equation via the marginal productivity conditions. It will reflect what we previously described as "commercial efficiency", viz. under- or over-shooting of the optimal capital-labour ratio for the given prices. For the regression equation to produce consistent estimates of ρ and δ, we require the relative price ratio to be independent of the disturbance term, that is, relative prices to be given to the individual firm. If the decision on relative factor inputs affects prices in factor markets (via the supply side), then simultaneous equation bias results. This will occur with any relatively high degree of aggregation. Feedback is less likely at the firm than the industry level, for individual firms are more likely to be price takers.

Having obtained $\hat{\delta}$ and $\hat{\rho}$, can the remaining parameters γ and ν be estimated? Write the production function as

$$Q = \gamma Z^{\nu} \quad \text{where} \quad Z = \{\delta K^{-\rho} + (1-\delta)L^{-\rho}\}^{-1/\rho}$$

An estimate $\hat{Z}$ can be constructed from estimates of ρ and δ and data on K and L. Then $\log Q = \log \gamma + \nu \log \hat{Z}$ can be estimated, provided that $\hat{Z}$ is independent of the error term which results from the "technical efficiency" disturbance in the production function. $\hat{Z}$ is a function not only of the K and L series but also of $\hat{\delta}$ and $\hat{\rho}$. Such estimates are always functions of the disturbance term in the regression equation they come from, so $\hat{\delta}$ and $\hat{\rho}$ are functions of the commercial efficiency disturbance. The two possible relationships between $\hat{Z}$ and the error term in the log Q regression can be dealt with by assuming (i) that technical efficiency is independent of commercial efficiency and so of $\hat{\delta}$ and $\hat{\rho}$, and (ii) that K and L are also independent of the technical efficiency disturbance.

Walters (1968, p.316) suggests that in the time series case $\hat{Z}$ and Q can also be used to derive an estimate of technical change (γ_t) as a residual in the Solow manner, i.e. $\hat{\gamma}_t = Q_t/\hat{Z}_t$. However, like the work of SMAC and Solow, this would assume constant returns. If $\nu \neq 1$ then the index of technical progress will be confused with the degree of homogeneity of the function.

Putting a trend term in the log $(\frac{K}{L})$ regression effectively allows $\frac{\delta}{1-\delta}$ (capital intensity) to vary over time - an example of a non-neutral technical change. A negative trend coefficient implies a declining $\frac{\delta}{1-\delta}$, that is capital saving technical progress. For the second stage of our regression we would then construct something like

$$\hat{Z} = \{\hat{\delta}\lambda^{t} K^{-\hat{\rho}} + (1-\hat{\delta}\lambda^{t})L^{-\hat{\rho}}\}^{-1/\hat{\rho}},$$

where λ is based on the estimated trend coefficient.

Identification problems are similar to those arising in the Cobb-Douglas case. If there is perfect competition, constant prices, and Q, K and L are endogenous, then the parameters of the three equation system are not identified. (For example the above regression equation for log $(\frac{K}{L})$ assumes variation in $\frac{w}{r}$ - if there is no such variation the equation cannot be estimated.) Nerlove (1967) suggests the following possibilities for identification. First, if all prices are exogenous but vary from observation to observation, Q, K and L being endogenous. Second, in the study of regulated industries, one might assume output also to be exogenous, the firm minimizing costs for a given output, with input prices varying across observations. Third, L, r and p might be taken to be the exogenous variables, which might be appropriate for inter-country comparisons when there is free trade, mobile capital, but immobile labour.

The major finding of Nerlove's survey is "the diversity of results: even slight variations in the period or concepts tend to produce drastically different estimates of the elasticity" of substitution. In his comment on the paper Mansfield extends this conclusion to cover estimates of the rate of technical progress. Their discussion is mainly concerned with the biases which may or may not occur under various economic and statistical specifications, and the difficulties which arise with various kinds of data. In addition to the aggregation problem which we passed by at the outset, we have seen that the specification problems are indeed considerable. Our discussion has served to illustrate the general identification and estimation problems in a specific area of application, and to indicate the difficulties which exist in empirically fleshing out the bare bones of this particular piece of economic theory. However the sophistication of the statistical methods is in sharp contrast to the simplicity of the concept of the production function, and subsequent progress may well require a re-examination of the underlying notion of the production function. One such reappraisal is to be found in the work of Johansen (1959, 1972), who replaces the traditional assumption of continuous substitution possibilities with the assumption that the firm's basic decision about factor proportions and the exploitation of new technologies is taken when investment in new plant and equipment occurs; subsequent decisions concern only the level of operation of the plant, current inputs being in fixed proportions to one another and to output. If such an approach is felt to be inapplicable to aggregate time series data except under very special circumstances, then perhaps as much is implied about the likely usefulness of an aggregate production function as about the relevance of the underlying model.

Chapter 3

THE INVESTMENT FUNCTION

Introduction

The main work to be studied in this chapter is that of Jorgenson and his co-workers, whose theory of investment behaviour is "based on the neoclassical theory of optimal accumulation of capital". Here, in the tradition of Irving Fisher, the firm acts to maximise its net worth, defined as the present value of all future net cash flows. Before discussing Jorgenson's work, and subsequently that of his critics, we first take a quick look at the more ad hoc tradition of investment studies, and then describe some generalisations of the simple geometric distributed lag function which have been applied in this field.

A starting point is provided by the accelerator model, which assumes that there is a fixed capital-output ratio α so that net investment is given by

$$\Delta K_t = \alpha \Delta Y_t .$$

However this simple form gives very poor results, and the regression estimate of α typically does not correspond at all closely to a capital-output ratio estimate. The flexible accelerator (or partial adjustment or stock adjustment hypothesis) provides a generalisation in which actual net investment is only a proportion of the investment required to achieve the desired capital stock position, K^*_t. Thus

$$K_t - K_{t-1} = (1-\lambda)(K^*_t - K_{t-1}).$$

If it is assumed that the capital-output ratio determines the desired capital stock, then

$$K^*_t = \alpha Y_t$$

and

$$K_t = \alpha(1-\lambda)Y_t + \lambda K_{t-1} .$$

This equation is equivalent to an expression for K_t as a distributed lag function of Y_t with geometrically declining coefficients,

$$K_t = \alpha(1-\lambda)\Sigma\lambda^j Y_{t-j} ,$$

and it was in this context that the original Koyck work (1954) was undertaken. As we shall see, investment theories differ according to (a) the determinants of the firm's desired capital stock position, and (b) the specification of adjustment process. A third element, on which there is almost complete agreement, is that of replacement investment.

Now gross investment is equal to net investment plus replacement investment:

$$I_t = \Delta K_t + D_t;$$

alternatively, end-period capital stock equals beginning capital stock plus gross investment less depreciation:

$$K_t = K_{t-1} + I_t - D_t .$$

The standard assumption is that replacement demand or depreciation is proportional to the existing stock:

$$D_t = \delta K_{t-1} ,$$

thus

$$I_t = K_t - (1-\delta)K_{t-1} .$$

This together with the partial adjustment hypothesis yields the following equation for gross investment:

$$I_t = (1-\lambda)K^*_t - (1-\lambda-\delta)K_{t-1} \; .$$

Such models have been used to study not only investment but also the demand for consumers' durable goods, when I_t represents purchases during period t and the desired stock depends on prices and consumers' income. For example, the studies in Harberger (1960), dealing with housing, refrigerators, automobiles, farm tractors, and corporate investment, are all of this type. In order to estimate the adjustment coefficient from a regression of I_t on K_{t-1} and the determinants of desired stock, an extraneous estimate of δ is required. This might be obtained from data on prices of new and second-hand goods or from information about the practice of accountants or tax assessors in calculating depreciation. If a direct estimate of δ is desired, or if stock data are not available, the equation can be transformed as follows:

$$\begin{aligned} I_t - (1-\delta)I_{t-1} &= (1-\lambda)\{K^*_t - (1-\delta)K^*_{t-1}\} \\ &\qquad - (1-\lambda-\delta)\{K_{t-1} - (1-\delta)K_{t-2}\} \\ &= (1-\lambda)\{K^*_t - (1-\delta)K^*_{t-1}\} - (1-\lambda-\delta)I_{t-1} \; , \end{aligned}$$

and so

$$I_t = (1-\lambda)K^*_t - (1-\lambda)(1-\delta)K^*_{t-1} + \lambda I_{t-1} \; .$$

If $K^*_t = \alpha Y_t$ as before, then a regression of I_t on Y_t, Y_{t-1}, and I_{t-1} will give estimates of α, λ, and δ. However, if K^*_t depends on two or more variables, say price p_t and income y_t in the case of consumer durables, then the underlying parameters will be overidentified. Writing

$$K^*_t = \alpha_1 p_t + \alpha_2 y_t \; ,$$

the regression equation has five coefficients (of p_t, y_t, p_{t-1}, y_{t-1}, and I_{t-1}) which are functions of four parameters (α_1, α_2, λ, and δ), and so unique parameter estimates cannot be deduced. This difficulty can be overcome by choosing a number of values of δ, then for each value constructing the series

$$p_t^{\dagger} = p_t - (1-\delta)p_{t-1} , \quad y_t^{\dagger} = y_t - (1-\delta)y_{t-1}$$

and estimating the regression

$$I_t = \alpha_1(1-\lambda)p_t^{\dagger} + \alpha_2(1-\lambda)y_t^{\dagger} + \lambda I_{t-1} ,$$

and finally selecting that value of δ which minimises the residual sum of squares. Estimates of α_1, α_2, and λ are then derived from the regression coefficients obtained with this value of δ. This method was suggested by Nerlove (1960) in the context of the study of expenditure on consumer durables by Stone and Rowe (1960).

Returning to the context of investment in physical capital, there are two main groups of variables which have been considered as relevant determinants of K^*. The use of output or sales in an accelerator framework has already been mentioned. Possible extensions are the use of expected or forecast sales in place of actual sales, the averaging of sales to eliminate short-run fluctuations, and corrections for the under-utilisation of capacity on the assumption that there is a fixed relation between K^* and potential output. The second group of determinants of K^* are financial variables, such as current or past levels of profits and the rate of return. Profits are relevant on the argument that investment is constrained by the supply of internal funds. What determines the level of investment is of importance for maintaining stability, promoting growth, and so forth, and the policy implications of the two groups of variables are different. For example if investment is a function of profits, then corporate taxes will be an important policy instrument. On the other hand, if investment depends on sales or demand expectations, corporate taxes will have little effect, and more appropriate instruments would be purchase taxes and demand stimulants. In practice, the justifications for either approach have been rather intuitive and rough-and-ready, and Jorgenson's model represented an important development, relating investment behaviour to profit maximising considerations. As a preliminary, we next discuss generalisations of the simple partial adjustment process.

Distributed lag functions

The general distributed lag model determining the variable y as a function of current and past values of the variable x, together with an error term, is

$$y_t = \sum_{j=0}^{\infty} \mu_j x_{t-j} + u_t.$$

Of course this representation, containing an infinite number of coefficients, has no empirical usefulness without further assumptions - it is simply a mathematically convenient general form.

One possibility is to postulate a maximum lag of m periods, say, after which a change in x has no effect on y. Thus $\mu_{m+1} = \mu_{m+2} = \ldots = 0$, and

$$y_t = \sum_{j=0}^{m} \mu_j x_{t-j} + u_t.$$

In principle, there is no difficulty in directly estimating the μ's, provided that the number of observations is greater than m. If the error term is independent of x and non-autocorrelated, then OLS will provide best, linear unbiased estimates. In practice, however, two difficulties are likely to arise. First, although m must be less than the sample size, it might still need to be relatively large, and so leave relatively few degrees of freedom for the estimation process. Second, irrespective of the behaviour of the error term, the x-variable is itself likely to be autocorrelated, resulting in multicollinearity problems - in particular, estimates of the μ's will tend to have large standard errors, and the general shape of the lag response function will not be very well determined. Consequently further assumptions about the shape of the lag distribution are necessary, in order to represent the m+1 coefficients as functions of a smaller number of parameters.

De Leeuw (1962) applied the "inverted *V*" lag distribution in which the coefficients increase linearly from $\mu_0 = 0$ to a peak at a lag of $m/2$ periods (assuming m even), and then decrease to zero at the same rate (this assumes $\mu_m = 0$). Thus, once the value of m is specified, there remains only one parameter to be estimated, for the lag distribution is completely determined by $\mu_m/2$, the height of the peak. In practice, different values of m were tried, and the value resulting in maximum R^2 chosen.

This approach is generalized by Almon (1965), who assumes that the lag distribution can be represented as a low-degree polynomial. Thus, writing the polynomial as

$$f(z) = a_0 + a_1 z + a_2 z^2 + \ldots + a_k z^k = \sum_{i=0}^{k} a_i z^i ,$$

the coefficients $\mu_0, \mu_1, \ldots, \mu_m$ are given by the values of $f(z)$ at the points $z = 0, 1, \ldots, m$, that is $\mu_j = \sum_{i=0}^{k} a_i j^i$. The number of parameters required to specify the distribution is then $k+1$, chosen to be rather less than the number of coefficients $m+1$. Making the substitution $\mu_j = f(j)$, the model becomes

$$\begin{aligned} y_t &= \sum_{j=0}^{m} \left(\sum_{i=0}^{k} a_i j^i \right) x_{t-j} + u_t \\ &= \sum_{i=0}^{k} a_i \left(\sum_{j=0}^{m} j^i x_{t-j} \right) + u_t , \end{aligned}$$

and so constructing new variables

$$x_{it} = \sum_{j=0}^{m} j^i x_{t-j} ,$$

the equation to be estimated is

$$y_t = \sum_{i=0}^{k} a_i x_{it} + u_t .$$

In practice, the construction of the new variables and the calculation of the $m+1$ μ-coefficients from the $k+1$ estimated a's is all carried out in widely-available computer packages. The degree of the polynomial, k, and the maximal lag, m, remain to be specified, so there is considerable scope for experimentation. Note that the polynomial $f(z)$ is only used in the range $0 \leq z \leq m$; outside this range the lag coefficients are specified to be zero, and the polynomial is not employed. However a further possibility, as applied by Almon, is to tie the lag distribution down by requiring the polynomial to give a zero value on either side, i.e. $f(-1) = f(m+1) = 0$ - these restrictions imply that only k-1 other parameters are required to specify the polynomial. But there is no particular reason to do this in general, and the evidence is that it tends to unnecessarily restrict the shape of the lag distribution; otherwise the range of possible shapes with a fourth-degree polynomial, as used by Almon, is quite wide. In estimating the distributed lag between capital appropriations and expenditures at the industry level, Almon's maximal lag varied between four and nine quarters.

After estimating either an inverted V or a polynomial lag structure, the hypothesis that the lag structure is of this form can be tested, using the residual sum of squares, under the maintained hypothesis that the maximal lag is m periods. This entails the computation of the residual sum of squares in an unrestricted multiple regression of y_t on $x_t, x_{t-1}, \ldots, x_{t-m}$ (without necessarily paying any attention to the coefficients), and a comparison with that obtained subject to the polynomial restriction. If the polynomial lag structure has a significantly higher residual sum of squares, then the data reject the restriction, and the polynomial hypothesis cannot be accepted. For some reason, this test is rarely carried out.

A second group of distributed lag specifications does not assume a finite maximal lag, but generalises the geometric lag structure, in which the coefficients approach zero asymptotically. In his own investment studies, Koyck (1954) assumed that the geometric decline began after the second coefficient, so that

$$y_t = \mu_0 x_t + \mu_1 x_{t-1} + \mu_1 \lambda x_{t-2} + \mu_1 \lambda^2 x_{t-3} + \ldots$$

and three parameters are required. Evans (1967) introduced a double distributed lag to account for modifications to original investment plans, and the time response of net investment to an increase in sales has the shape of an inverted *W*. The first peak occurs at a lag of one quarter, the coefficients decline for three quarters, the second peak occurs at a six-quarter lag, then the geometric decline sets in. To discuss further generalisations, it is convenient to introduce lag operator notation.

The lag operator L is defined by

$$Lx_t = x_{t-1}$$

and with repeated application, we have

$$L^j x_t = x_{t-j} \; .$$

The advantage of this approach is that we can carry out algebraic operations with L as if it were an ordinary variable. Thus

$$L^j L^k = L^{j+k}$$

since both applied to x_t give x_{t-j-k} , and if a_1, a_2 are constants, then

$$L^j(a_1 x_{1t} + a_2 x_{2t}) = a_1 L^j x_{1t} + a_2 L^j x_{2t} = a_1 x_{1,t-j} + a_2 x_{2,t-j} \; .$$

The general lag function can now be written

$$\Sigma \mu_j x_{t-j} = \Sigma \mu_j L^j x_t = \mu(L) x_t$$

where $\mu(L)$ is the (unrestricted) polynomial in L

$$\mu(L) = \mu_0 + \mu_1 L + \mu_2 L^2 + \dots \; .$$

As far as reciprocals and division are concerned, by $\frac{1}{L} x_t$ we mean that variable which yields x_t when L is applied, namely x_{t+1} , and by $\frac{1}{\mu(L)} y_t$ we mean that variable which results in y_t when $\mu(L)$ is applied. Thus, if

$$y_t = \mu(L)x_t \quad \text{then} \quad \frac{1}{\mu(L)}y_t = x_t.$$

The Koyck transformation for the case of geometrically declining coefficients can be easily cast in this framework. Assuming $\mu_j = \beta\lambda^j$, we have

$$\begin{aligned} y_t &= \beta\Sigma\lambda^j x_{t-j} + u_t = \beta\Sigma\lambda^j L^j x_t + u_t \\ &= \beta(1+\lambda L+\lambda^2 L^2+\lambda^3 L^3+\dots)\, x_t + u_t \\ &= \frac{\beta}{1-\lambda L}x_t + u_t \quad \text{if} \quad |\lambda| < 1 \end{aligned}$$

applying the formula for the sum of a geometric series. Multiplying through by $(1-\lambda L)$ gives

$$(1-\lambda L)y_t = \beta x_t + (1-\lambda L)u_t$$

that is, as before,

$$y_t = \lambda y_{t-1} + \beta x_t + (u_t - \lambda u_{t-1}).$$

Jorgenson (1963 *et seq.*) approximates the general infinite distributed lag function by a ratio of two finite polynomials in L. It is assumed that

$$\mu(L) = \frac{\gamma(L)}{\omega(L)} = \frac{\gamma_0+\gamma_1 L + \dots + \gamma_k L^k}{\omega_0+\omega_1 L + \dots + \omega_l L^l},$$

and this is referred to as the <u>rational lag function</u>. Any lag function can be approximated by a rational lag function as closely as we like by making k and/or l sufficiently large. This generalises the schemes discussed so far: the Almon lag structure is obtained when $\omega(L) = 1$ and the γ-coefficients are suitably restricted, and the geometric lag structure is given by $\gamma(L) = \beta$, $\omega(L) = 1-\lambda L$ (i.e. k=0, l=1). The generalisation of the Koyck transformation is immediate, for if

$$y_t = \frac{\gamma(L)}{\omega(L)} x_t + u_t$$

then

$$\omega(L)y_t = \gamma(L)x_t + \omega(L)u_t.$$

(The conventional normalisation rule is to set $\omega_0=1$.) The estimating equation contains l lagged values of the dependent variable and k lagged values of the explanatory variable, and has an error term which is an l-order moving average of the original disturbance term. Thus if u_t is independent, $\omega(L)u_t$ is autocorrelated, and OLS will provide inconsistent estimates, so alternative estimators may be required.

Finally, we illustrate operations with polynomials in L by looking at multiplication and division. The net effect of the successive application of two polynomials in L to a given series is evaluated by calculating their product or "convolution". If $\gamma(L)$ and $\omega(L)$ are of degree k and l respectively as above, then applying both to a given series will produce a maximum lag of $k+l$ periods, and their product $\alpha(L)$ is a polynomial in L of degree $k+l$:

$$\alpha(L) = \gamma(L)\omega(L).$$

The two polynomials on either side of this equation are equivalent if the coefficients of each separate power of L correspond, so the α-coefficients are obtained by picking out the coefficients of particular powers of L on the right hand side. We have

$$(\alpha_0+\alpha_1 L+\alpha_2 L^2 + \ldots + \alpha_{l+k} L^{l+k}) = (\gamma_0+\gamma_1 L + \ldots + \gamma_k L^k)(\omega_0+\omega_1 L + \ldots + \omega_l L^l)$$

and equating coefficients gives

$$\begin{aligned}
\text{constant term:}\quad & \alpha_0 = \gamma_0\omega_0 \\
\text{coefficient of L:}\quad & \alpha_1 = \gamma_0\omega_1+\gamma_1\omega_0 \\
\text{coefficient of } L^2\text{:}\quad & \alpha_2 = \gamma_0\omega_2+\gamma_1\omega_1+\gamma_2\omega_0 \\
\vdots\quad & \vdots \\
\text{coefficient of } L^{l+k}\text{:}\quad & \alpha_{l+k} = \gamma_k\omega_l.
\end{aligned}$$

Thus the joint effect of two or more polynomials in L can be easily calculated.

We consider division of polynomials in L by asking how the μ-coefficients in the rational lag function $\mu(L) = \gamma(L)/\omega(L)$ can be calculated from the given polynomials $\gamma(L)$ and $\omega(L)$. One approach is to factorise $\omega(L)$ and so express $1/\omega(L)$ in partial fractions, and then obtain a power series expansion for each term separately - $\mu(L)$ is in general of infinite degree, although we shall require that $\mu_j \to 0$ as $j \to \infty$. The following illustration uses numbers similar to those obtained by Jorgenson, who typically took $l=2$, thus adding one extra lagged value of the dependent variable to the Koyck equation. Taking

$$\omega(L) = (1 - 1.25\ L + .375\ L^2),$$

the coefficients of the lagged dependent variables, when written on the right hand side of the equation, are 1.25 and -.375. We require the reciprocal of this, expressed in terms of positive powers of L, so that we can interpret $\frac{1}{\omega(L)}x_t$. First, $\omega(L)$ is factorized, giving

$$\omega(L) = (1 - .75\ L)(1 - .5\ L).$$

Then, applying the method of partial fractions, we write

$$\frac{1}{\omega(L)} = \frac{1}{(1-\frac{3}{4}L)(1-\frac{1}{2}L)} = \frac{A}{1-\frac{3}{4}L} + \frac{B}{1-\frac{1}{2}L}$$

and solve for A and B by comparing the numerators when the third term is put over a common denominator. Thus

$$\frac{1}{(1-\frac{3}{4}L)(1-\frac{1}{2}L)} = \frac{A(1-\frac{1}{2}L)+B(1-\frac{3}{4}L)}{(1-\frac{3}{4}L)(1-\frac{1}{2}L)}$$

and the two sides are equivalent if the numerators match up. Since the numerator on the left contains a constant and no power of L, we require

$$1 = A + B \quad \text{and} \quad 0 = -\tfrac{1}{2}A - \tfrac{3}{4}B$$

hence $A = 3$ and $B = -2$, or

$$\frac{1}{\omega(L)} = \frac{3}{1-\frac{3}{4}L} - \frac{2}{1-\frac{1}{2}L} .$$

We can now express this as a power series in L by the usual binomial expansion, reversing the operation of summing a geometric series, that is,

$$\frac{1}{\omega(L)} = 3\{1 + \tfrac{3}{4}L + (\tfrac{3}{4}L)^2 + (\tfrac{3}{4}L)^3 + \ldots\} - 2\{1 + \tfrac{1}{2}L + \tfrac{1}{4}L^2 + \tfrac{1}{8}L^3 + \ldots\}.$$

Calculating the first few coefficients gives

$$\frac{1}{\omega(L)} = 1 + 1.25\,L + 1.1875\,L^2 + 1.0156\,L^3 + .8242\,L^4 + .6494\,L^5 + .5027\,L^6 + \ldots$$

We see that the coefficients are made up of increasing powers of $\frac{3}{4}$ and $\frac{1}{2}$, and so tend to zero. It is only when the coefficients of increasing powers of L do approach zero asymptotically that the inverse polynomial has a well-defined meaning. The condition for this to hold is that when $\omega(L)$ is factorized, the coefficient of L in each factor should lie between -1 and 1, as indeed they do in our example. The requirement that these coefficients are less than 1 in absolute value generalises the requirement that $|\lambda| < 1$ in first order, Koyck models and ensures that the difference equation $\omega(L)y_t = a$ is stable. Lastly $\mu(L) = \gamma(L)/\omega(L)$ is obtained by multiplying this expression for $1/\omega(L)$ by $\gamma(L)$ using the method of the previous paragraph. Since $\gamma(L)$ is of finite degree and has finite coefficients, it will not affect these stability or convergence properties, so the condition on the factors of $\omega(L)$ is sufficient to ensure that $\mu_j \to 0$ as $j \to \infty$.

An alternative approach to calculating the coefficients in $\mu(L) = \gamma(L)/\omega(L)$ is to write down the relations between coefficients resulting from the equation $\gamma(L) = \omega(L)\mu(L)$, as follows ($\omega_0 = 1$):

$$\gamma_0 = \mu_0$$
$$\gamma_1 = \mu_0\omega_1 + \mu_1$$
$$\gamma_2 = \mu_0\omega_2 + \mu_1\omega_1 + \mu_2$$

and so on, ad infinitun. Given the ω's and γ's, these equations can then be solved recursively for the μ's.

In the general distributed lag model

$$y_t = \Sigma\mu_j x_{t-j} + u_t$$

the <u>total multiplier</u>, giving the change in the equilibrium value of y in response to a unit increase in the level of x, is $\Sigma\mu_j$. This is easily calculated from the γ- and ω-coefficients of the rational lag function, for the required sum is given by evaluating the polynomials at 1. Thus

$$\mu_0 + \mu_1 + \mu_2 + \ldots = \mu(1) = \gamma(1)/\omega(1),$$

and we simply take the ratio of the sums of the γ- and ω-coefficients. In our reciprocal polynomial example, the sum of the infinite series of coefficients, of which the first seven are given above, is $(1 - 1.25 + .375)^{-1} = 8$.

The Jorgenson model

The basic hypothesis used by Jorgenson (1963, 1965, 1967) is that the firm maximises its net worth, that is the present value of future net revenues. Net revenue is equal to income less outlay on current account less outlay on capital account:

$$R(t) = p(t)Q(t) - s(t)L(t) - q(t)I(t),$$

where $Q(t)$ is the amount of output and $p(t)$ its price, $L(t)$ is the amount of labour (or variable) input and $s(t)$ its price, $I(t)$ is the volume of gross investment and $q(t)$ the price of capital goods. This notation comprises three elements - a single output, a single variable input and a single capital input - which are continuously variable over time, and there is no investment in stocks of finished goods, for sales are equal to output. At the market interest rate or discount rate r, the present value of all future net revenues of the firm is

$$W = \int_0^{\infty} e^{-rt} R(t)dt.$$

Basically, net worth is being calculated at a particular point in time, and the net worth of time t would be more generally written as

$$W(t) = \int_t^{\infty} e^{-r(\tau-t)} R(\tau)d\tau.$$

Net worth is maximized subject to two constraints.
(i) Output and inputs are constrained by the production function, which is assumed to have all the neo-classical properties. Jorgenson writes it in implicit form, $F_1\{Q(t), L(t), K(t)\} = 0$ or equivalently, we can write $Q(t) = F\{K(t), L(t)\}$ as in Chapter 2. In due course the Cobb-Douglas specification will be adopted.
(ii) The second constraint is on the behaviour of the investment series, namely that total investment is equal to net investment plus depreciation:

$$I(t) = \dot{K}(t) + \delta K(t).$$

$\dot{K}(t) = \frac{d}{dt}K(t)$ is the rate of change of the capital stock, and the $\delta K(t)$ term incorporates the proportionate depreciation assumption - capital is homogeneous and there are no vintage effects.

The problem now is to maximise the present value of the firm subject to the production function and the investment relationship. Consider the Lagrangean:

$$\mathcal{L} = \int_0^{\infty} \left(e^{-rt} R(t) + \lambda_0(t)\{Q(t)-F[K(t),L(t)]\} + \lambda_1(t)\{\dot{K}(t)-I(t)+\delta K(t)\}\right)dt.$$

All variables are continuous functions of time, thus prices are assumed to vary continuously and not to behave like step functions; also investment is continuously variable - there is no capacity constraint or lumpiness. Writing the Lagrange multipliers as functions of time implies that the constraints must be satisfied in every time period. We can abbreviate to

$$\mathcal{L} = \int_0^\infty f(t)dt$$

where

$$f(t) = e^{-rt}\{p(t)Q(t)-s(t)L(t)-q(t)I(t)\} + \lambda_0(t)\{Q(t)-F[K(t),L(t)]\}$$

$$+ \lambda_1(t)\{\dot{K}(t)-I(t)+\delta K(t)\}.$$

The main problem is that in this function we have not only the variables with respect to which we are maximizing, but also the time derivatives of some of those variables. That is $\mathcal{L} = \int f(x,t,\dot{x})dt$. Basically, the standard first-order conditions need slightly modifying, and this involves the calculus of variations. The problem which causes links between different time periods is the rate of change variable, so it is not enough simply to maximise f with respect to x in every time period. The required procedure follows from Euler's equation (a necessary condition) which is a slight generalisation of the standard first-order condition for an extreme value. All we require is that the usual first derivative is modified by subtracting from it the time derivative of the first derivative with respect to the rate of change variable and the condition becomes $\frac{\partial f}{\partial x} - \frac{d}{dt}(\frac{\partial f}{\partial \dot{x}}) = 0$. (See for example Allen, 1938, Ch. 20).

Differentiating with respect to Q, L, I presents no problem, since their rates of change are not involved. Dropping the time variable for convenience but remembering that prices, quantities and λ's are functions of time we have:

$$(1)\ \frac{\partial f}{\partial Q} = e^{-rt}p + \lambda_0 = 0$$

$$(2)\ \frac{\partial f}{\partial L} = -e^{-rt}s - \lambda_0\frac{\partial F}{\partial L} = 0$$

$$(3)\ \frac{\partial f}{\partial I} = -e^{-rt}q - \lambda_1 = 0$$

Setting the first derivative with respect to λ_0 equal to zero ensures that the production function is satisfied in every time period, and this together with equations (1) and (2) gives the usual marginal productivity condition for L:

$$\frac{\partial Q}{\partial L} = \frac{s}{p} .$$

The final first-order condition makes use of Euler's equation:

$$\frac{\partial f}{\partial K} - \frac{d}{dt}\left(\frac{\partial f}{\partial \dot{K}}\right) = - \lambda_0 \frac{\partial F}{\partial K} + \lambda_1 \delta - \frac{d}{dt} \lambda_1(t) = 0.$$

From (3) we have $\lambda_1 = -e^{-rt} q$ and so

$$\frac{d\lambda_1}{dt} = rqe^{-rt} - \dot{q}e^{-rt} ,$$

hence

$$-\lambda_0 \frac{\partial F}{\partial K} - q\delta e^{-rt} - rqe^{-rt} + \dot{q}e^{-rt} = 0.$$

Finally, substituting for λ_0 from (1), and remembering that $Q = F(K,L)$, we obtain

$$\frac{\partial Q}{\partial K} = \frac{q(r+\delta)-\dot{q}}{p} = \frac{c}{p}.$$

The result is the marginal productivity condition for capital services, where c is the implicit rental value of capital services. Jorgenson refers to this as "user cost", although as Tobin (1967) comments, in Keynes' terminology user cost is the "reduction in value of equipment due to using it as compared to not using it" and the fall in value of equipment depends on the intensity of use. These effects are absent in Jorgenson's work, where c is an ownership cost. Capital services are purchased at market rental, assuming perfect competition and a perfect market in capital goods. As a simple discrete-time illustration of what is going on, consider the cost of using one machine for one time period. Funds are borrowed to purchase the machine at a price of q_t, and the cost of these funds over the period is rq_t. At the end of the period only (1-δ) of the machine is left, which is sold at the price q_{t+1}. So the cost is $q_t + rq_t - (1-\delta)q_{t+1}$, i.e. $c \simeq q(r+\delta)-\Delta q$, equal to the cost of funds plus depreciation less capital gains.

<u>Taxation</u> is often introduced into the model, permitting the study of the effect on investment of changing tax parameters. Net worth is redefined as the present value of revenue net of taxes:

$$W = \int_0^\infty e^{-rt} \{R(t) - T(t)\}dt.$$

It is assumed that income tax is charged at some rate u $(0 \leq u \leq 1)$ on gross income less outlay on current account and certain capital allowances where

v is the proportion of depreciation $q\delta K$ deductible,

w is the proportion of interest payments rqK deductible,

x is the proportion of capital gains qK chargeable.

Then the tax function is

$$T(t) = u\{pQ - sL - vq\delta K - wrqK + x\dot{q}K\} = u\{pQ - sL - q(v\delta + wr - x\frac{\dot{q}}{q})K\}.$$

The effect of introducing this is to convert c into an 'after tax' cost:

$$c = q\{(\frac{1-uv}{1-u})\delta + (\frac{1-uw}{1-u})r\} - (\frac{1-ux}{1-u})\dot{q}.$$

Each of the factors such as $(\frac{1-uv}{1-u})$ is greater than 1 unless v, w, x = 1. That is, c is increased unless all depreciation and interest is tax deductible.

A Cobb-Douglas production function is assumed with $\alpha + \beta < 1$, making the firm's size determinate in a purely competitive world. Then the marginal productivity conditions become

$$\frac{\partial Q}{\partial L} = \beta\frac{Q}{L} = \frac{s}{p}, \quad \frac{\partial Q}{\partial K} = \alpha\frac{Q}{K} = \frac{c}{p},$$

and these, together with the function $Q = AK^{\alpha}L^{\beta}$, determine the levels of output, labour and capital inputs. Demand for investment goods is then given by $I = \dot{K} + \delta K$.

Although these conditions hold at all points in time, the model at this point is not very dynamic. The firm has solved an essentially static optimization problem, and the only link between time periods is the capital stock series. Nevertheless, the model is noteworthy for basing the demand for investment goods on profit maximising considerations. It also provides a description of the relationship between the demand for capital goods and the given technology via the production function, and a derivation of the relevant price of capital services, depending on the interest rate, the price of capital goods, and so forth. In translating this description of the demand for capital goods into an explanation of investment expenditures over time, Jorgenson adds an adjustment mechanism to account for the fact that investment projects take time to complete, hence instantaneous achievement of the optimal capital stock position is not possible. There are lags in the delivery of new machines, and so orders placed today will only be delivered at some future point in time. Although Jorgenson's handling of the resulting distributed lag in terms of a rational lag function is a considerable generalisation of the partial adjustment hypothesis, the justification for the distributed lag seems no less ad hoc. (General expectations models are equally possible.)

At time t, the marginal productivity condition for capital gives

$$K_t^* = \alpha \frac{p_t Q_t}{c_t}$$

as the desired or equilibrium stock, but the actual stock K_t differs from this due to past delays in installing new equipment, and cannot be immediately adjusted to the desired figure. So the assumption is that Q and L are determined by the production function and the marginal productivity condition for labour, given the stock of capital. The marginal productivity condition for capital then determines the desired stock K^*, and orders are placed sufficient to achieve K^* by the time they are delivered. The firm attempts to adjust instantaneously, but is thwarted by unanticipated delivery lags.

Let new investment projects initiated or orders placed in period t for expansion of capacity (not replacement) be IN_t. In the last period (t-1) the firm ordered sufficient to achieve K^*_{t-1} by the time all new orders are delivered. So given that the procedure is well-established, in this period the firm only has to order enough new machines to make up the difference between the current and previous desired levels:

$$IN_t = K^*_t - K^*_{t-1} = \Delta K^*_t .$$

As investment projects take time to complete, let μ_j be the proportion which takes j periods to complete. Then of orders placed this period, a proportion μ_0 will be delivered immediately, a proportion μ_1 will be delivered in the next period, μ_2 in the period after that, and so on. If all orders are delivered (no bankruptcies among suppliers or cancellations) then $\sum_{j=0}^{\infty} \mu_j = 1$. The consequence is that current investment expenditure, IE_t, for expansion of capacity is a function of past orders and has the same coefficients, for a proportion μ_0 of current orders are delivered this period, a proportion μ_1 of the orders placed last period will be delivered in the current period, μ_2 of the orders placed two periods ago will also be delivered this period, and so on. Thus

$$IE_t = \sum_{j=0}^{\infty} \mu_j IN_{t-j} = \sum_{j=0}^{\infty} \mu_j \Delta K^*_{t-j} ,$$

and actual investment expenditure is a distributed lag function of current and past orders, or changes in desired capital stock. These delivery delays are assumed constant, so that if orders are (say) quadrupled, a proportion μ_0 is still delivered immediately, μ_1 in the next period, etc. If ΔK^*_t is negative the firm may start selling capital equipment, but its behaviour then is not described by this same distributed lag, so there is an assumption that $\Delta K^*_t > 0$.

Gross investment has two components:

$$I_t = IE_t + IR_t = \Delta K_t + \delta K_{t-1}$$

where IR_t is replacement investment, assumed to be proportional to the beginning capital stock K_{t-1}. Accordingly we now have

$$I_t = \sum_{j=0}^{\infty} \mu_j IN_{t-j} + IR_t = \sum_{j=0}^{\infty} \mu_j \Delta K^*_{t-j} + \delta K_{t-1} .$$

Finally, incorporating the determinants of desired capital stock, we obtain an equation for net investment, as follows:

$$I_t - \delta K_{t-1} = \sum_{j=0}^{\infty} \mu_j \Delta\left(\alpha\frac{pQ}{c}\right)_{t-j} .$$

Estimation of the Jorgenson investment function

At this point, the rational lag function is employed. Writing the model in the form

$$I_t - \delta K_{t-1} = \mu(L)\Delta\left(\alpha\frac{pQ}{c}\right)_t ,$$

then substituting $\mu(L) = \gamma(L)/\omega(L)$ and multiplying through by $\omega(L)$ gives

$$\omega(L)\{I_t - \delta K_{t-1}\} = \gamma(L)\Delta\left(\alpha\frac{pQ}{c}\right)_t .$$

Generally Jorgenson takes $\omega(L)$ to be a second-degree polynomial (i.e. $l = 2$), normalised by setting $\omega_0 = 1$, so the equation becomes

$$I_t - \delta K_{t-1} = \alpha\gamma(L)\Delta\left(\frac{pQ}{c}\right)_t - \omega_1(I_{t-1} - \delta K_{t-2}) - \omega_2(I_{t-2} - \delta K_{t-3}),$$

and a constant term is also added. In the first work (Jorgenson, 1963) $\gamma(L)$ has only one non-zero coefficient, γ_2, but in the next reference (Jorgenson, 1965) there are up to three non-zero coefficients,

$\gamma(L)$ for total durables manufacturing, for example, being $\gamma_3 L^3 + \gamma_4 L^4 + \gamma_5 L^5$. In this latter case a change in one of the determinants of K^* at a given point of time does not start to affect investment expenditures until three quarters later - generally quarterly data are employed. There are few formal criteria available to guide the choice of particular lag polynomials, and Jorgenson relies on the estimated standard error of the regression together with certain general restrictions derived from exploratory empirical research - in later work the degree of $\gamma(L)$ is limited to seven, with at most four non-zero coefficients, these being adjacent to one another, with the first coefficient positive.

As usual the derived equation will not fit the observations exactly so a disturbance term is added. Unfortunately Jorgenson provides no rationalisation for the disturbances (e.g. failures of profit maximisation, random variation in delivery times) but simply adds a general catch-all term to the estimating equation - no explanation is provided in terms of errors in the component structural equations of the model. Notice that if we add a disturbance u_t to the original investment equation $I_t - \delta K_{t-1} = \frac{\gamma(L)}{\omega(L)}\Delta K^*_t$ then in multiplying through by $\omega(L)$ we obtain

$$\omega(L)(I_t - \delta K_{t-1}) = \gamma(L)\Delta K^*_t + \omega(L)u_t$$

and it is this error term in the final equation which is assumed independent, i.e. $\omega(L)u_t = \varepsilon_t$. If this assumption (that the original u_t has the autoregressive structure $u_t + \omega_1 u_{t-1} + \omega_2 u_{t-2} = \varepsilon_t$ with the same ω-coefficients) is correct, then estimation can proceed by ordinary least squares. But if the original error term is independent, the multiplication by $\omega(L)$ will induce autocorrelation in the final error term, and ordinary least squares estimates will be inconsistent. The Durbin-Watson test was not designed for equations containing lagged values of the dependent variable, so it is not possible to use this test for autocorrelation - when the lagged dependent variable is present on the right hand side the Durbin-Watson statistic is biased towards 2.

The capital stock series has to be constructed using data on I_t, an assumed value of δ, and the relation

$$K_t = I_t + (1-\delta)K_{t-1} ,$$

for while benchmark observations on capital stock are available from Censuses of Production, quarterly data are not available. An estimate of δ is obtained by using this recursion relation and the investment series to interpolate between two capital stock benchmark figures - in the first work this gave a value of 0.025. There are now the alternative possibilities of leaving δK_{t-1} as part of the dependent variable or of taking it to the right hand side; in the latter case a regression estimate of δ is obtained together with the other coefficients. Jorgenson calls the former situation, where $-\delta K_{t-1}$ remains as part of the dependent variable with the value of δ obtained as above, the restricted case. The unrestricted case provides an estimate which is not constrained to equal 0.025, by estimating δ as the coefficient of K_{t-1} . The value obtained in this way can be used as a rough check on the value of δ used in calculating the capital stock series. However, the test is not a particularly strong one, since the assumed value of the depreciation parameter is built into the capital stock series, and one would not expect the estimated value to be far from it, no matter how inappropriate it was.

Finally, the exponent α in the Cobb-Douglas production function is estimated from the requirement that $\Sigma\mu_j = 1$. We have estimates of ω's and $(\alpha\gamma)$'s, and the sum of the μ-coefficients is set equal to one by requiring that $\hat{\gamma}(1)/\hat{\omega}(1) = 1$, hence

$$\hat{\alpha} = \frac{\widehat{\alpha\gamma}(1)}{\hat{\omega}(1)} = \frac{\text{sum of coefficients on } \Delta(\frac{pQ}{c}) \text{ terms}}{1 + \hat{\omega}_1 + \hat{\omega}_2}$$

A simple illustration is provided by Jorgenson (1963), using data on total manufacturing (restricted case):

$$(I_t - \delta K_{t-1}) = \text{constant} + \underset{(0.099)}{1.524}\,(I_{t-1} - \delta K_{t-2}) - \underset{(0.101)}{0.631}\,(I_{t-2} - \delta K_{t-3})$$

$$+ \underset{(0.0005)}{0.00106}\,\Delta\frac{p_{t-2}\,Q_{t-2}}{c_{t-2}} \qquad R^2 = 0.942 \quad DW = 2.11$$

By standard statistical criteria these results are good though the *DW* statistic must be taken with a pinch of salt. The estimated lag functions are

$$\hat{\omega}(L) = 1 - 1.524\,L + 0.631\,L^2 \quad \text{and} \quad \alpha\hat{\gamma}(L) = 0.00106\,L^2$$

hence $\hat{\alpha} = \dfrac{0.00106}{0.107} = 0.01$, which seems on the low side.

Since the programme of work began the emphasis has been on disaggregating the data. Jorgenson (1965) breaks total manufacturing into durables and non-durables and later work has applied the same model to 15 sub-industries of total manufacturing. (Jorgenson and Stephenson, (1967a, 1967b, 1969a) - the first paper contains the regression results and the second concentrates upon the implied μ's; the third is concerned with anticipations data, discussed below.) Jorgenson and Stephenson defend their small estimates of α by arguing that the estimated value would correspond to the relative share of capital in value added (cf. p.34) only where desired and actual capital were equal. A supplementary defence is that downward bias may result from measurement errors in observed values of changes in desired capital. In general, these results suggest that production function parameters should be estimated from this investment theory only if the accuracy of the definition and measurement of desired capital can be improved. In any case, simultaneity problems are by no means absent, as we shall see.

Nevertheless the results provide some support for the neoclassical view that capital prices affect investment decisions, although the influence of each element of *p/c* cannot be distinguished. The effects of interest rates, taxation and so forth can be derived from the estimates, together with the paths of dynamic response to changes, by using $\hat{\alpha}$ to obtain $\hat{\gamma}(L)/\hat{\omega}(L)$ and then deriving $\hat{\mu}(L)$ as illustrated on p. 74. An average lag between a change in the demand for capital stock and the corresponding net investment can be calculated as $\Sigma j\mu_j$, which is estimated at $6\frac{1}{2}$ quarters. The first non-zero value of the μ's is μ_2 in this example; a typical distribution is sketched in Figure 10.

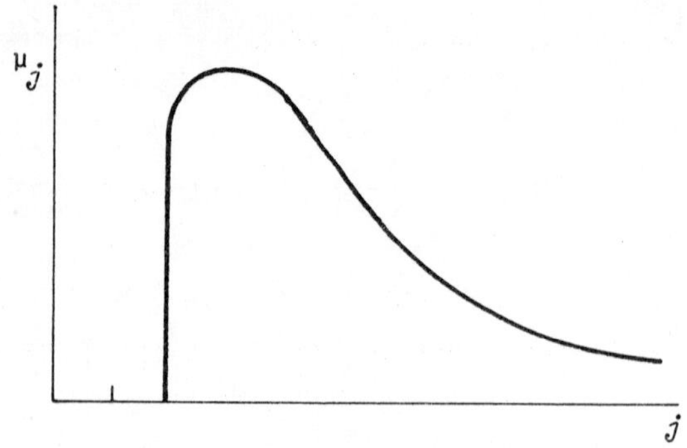

Figure 10

Stages of the process

If data on intermediate stages of the investment process are available, then it is of interest to disaggregate the lags between changes in the determinants of the desired capital stock and consequential changes in investment expenditures. The following sequence is envisaged. Output price, the interest rate or some other determinant of K^*, x say, changes. That leads to an appropriation of funds (y_1) which subsequently causes new orders or contracts (y_2). In due course this sequence leads to a change in investment expenditure (y). The sort of data that may be available on these intermediate stages typically arises from intentions surveys and it may be that, for instance, one gets better forecasts using data on an intermediate stage rather than going back to the original determinants. The whole process can be summarised in

$$y_t = \mu(L)x_t$$

which says as usual that investment depends on lagged values of the determinants of desired capital stock, but the process can be broken down by representing each stage as a function of the one preceding it, as follows:

$$y_{1t} = \nu_0(L)x_t, \quad y_{2t} = \nu_1(L)y_{1t}, \quad y_t = \nu_2(L)y_{2t}.$$

In order for the lag distributions to be consistent the general relation between y and x must be obtained as the product of the three separate distributed lag functions:

$$\mu(L) = \nu_0(L)\nu_1(L)\nu_2(L).$$

If the appropriate data are available tests of the agreement between the separate functions can be performed.

Jorgenson (1965) and Jorgenson and Stephenson (1969a) use this formulation to explain investment anticipations one and two quarters ahead ($IA(1)$ and $IA(2)$, equal to y_2 and y_1 respectively in our illustraction). By expressing any later stage as a distributed lag function of any earlier stage six regressions are possible, which can be checked for internal consistency. For example,

$$I_t = \nu_2(L)IA(1)_t = \nu_2(L)\nu_1(L)IA(2)_t, \quad IA(2)_t = \nu_0(L)\Delta K^*_t + \delta K_{t-1},$$

and so on. In practice $\nu_1(L)$ and $\nu_2(L)$ have only the first order term, comprising a coefficient times L, and $\nu_0(L)$ is of the rational form discussed above, with a second degree polynomial in the denominator. When the estimated products $\nu_1\nu_0$ and $\mu = \nu_2\nu_1\nu_0$ and so on are compared, good agreement is generally obtained (that is, in comparing $\widehat{\nu_2\nu_1}$ with $\hat{\nu}_2\hat{\nu}_1$, say). This is not too surprising given that the forms of the polynomials are specified a priori to be compatible with one another - in estimating ν_0, or $\nu_1\nu_0$, or $\nu_2\nu_1\nu_0$ a second degree denominator is always used, and the starting points of the numerator lag polynomials are kept in agreement. Thus it is not surprising that such statistics as the average lag appear consistent, for the only things remaining to check are the numerical values of the corresponding coefficients - here the agreement is generally good.

Structure of the investment process

We are now in a position to use the estimates to relate investment to alternative policy instruments and other influences. To do so we need to study the effect of changes in K^*_t on actual (gross) investment expenditures (I_t) over time. For example, we may study the pattern of response in order to discover what sort of countercyclical policy will be stabilising. Starting from the standard equation

$$I_t = \mu(L)\Delta K^*_t + \delta K_{t-1} ,$$

and given the distribution $\mu(L)$, we can derive a final equation which relates I_t directly to the determinants of K^*_t and so allows for replacement effects by solving out the δK_{t-1} term. The equation $I_t = \Delta K_t + \delta K_{t-1}$ can be rewritten as

$$I_t = \{1 - (1-\delta)L\}K_t,$$

and it can also be substituted in the first equation to obtain

$$\Delta K_t = \mu(L)\Delta K^*_t, \quad \text{or} \quad K_t = \mu(L)K^*_t.$$

Hence

$$I_t = \{1 - (1-\delta)L\}\mu(L)K^*_t$$

$$= \eta(L)K^*_t,$$

where $\eta(L) = \eta_0+\eta_1L+\eta_2L^2+ \ldots$ is another polynomial in L.

Suppose that K^* has been constant for some time, but it then changes to new level, following a change in an interest rate or a tax parameter, for example. Then the coefficient η_0 gives the instantaneous response of I_t and, assuming the change is maintained, $\eta_0+\eta_1$ the effect on I_t one period later, $\eta_0+\eta_1+\eta_2$ the effect two periods later, and so on. Notice that the effect cumulates as I picks up to its new level. Hence we need partial sums of these coefficients to describe the path of investment. The η's are given in terms of the known μ's and δ by

$$\eta_0+\eta_1L+\eta_2L^2+\eta_3L^3 + \ldots = \{1-(1-\delta)L\}\{\mu_0+\mu_1L+\mu_2L^2+ \ldots\},$$

and so by equating coefficients of powers of L we have

$$\eta_0=\mu_0, \quad \eta_1=\mu_1-(1-\delta)\mu_0, \quad \eta_2=\mu_2-(1-\delta)\mu_1, \text{ etc.}$$

The partial sums ξ_τ giving the effect on I of a change in K^* after τ periods are thus

$$\xi_\tau = \sum_{j=0}^{\tau} \eta_j = \sum_{j=0}^{\tau} \mu_j - (1-\delta) \sum_{j=0}^{\tau-1} \mu_j$$

$$= \mu_\tau + \delta \sum_{j=0}^{\tau-1} \mu_j .$$

Recalling that μ_j represents the proportion of orders which are delivered after j periods, we expect that $\mu_j \to 0$ as $j \to \infty$; also all orders are delivered at some time, so $\sum_{j=0}^{\tau} \mu_j \to 1$ as $\tau \to \infty$. It therefore follows that

$$\xi_\tau \to \delta \quad \text{as} \quad \tau \to \infty,$$

that is, a change in K^* has a long-run effect equal to the replacement proportion. If K^* increases to a higher level, and subsequently investment occurs to adjust actual K to K^*, then once this is achieved replacement investment is all that is occurring, and this is higher than before by a proportion δ of the increase in K^* (and K).

To assess the effect on gross investment expenditures of an interest rate change we seek

$$\frac{\partial I}{\partial r} = \frac{\partial I}{\partial K^*} \frac{\partial K^*}{\partial r}$$

and $\xi_\tau \frac{\partial K^*}{\partial r}$ gives the effect τ periods later - the long run effect is $\delta \frac{\partial K^*}{\partial r}$.

Recall that $K^* = \alpha \frac{pQ}{c}$, with c a function of r, hence $\frac{\partial K^*}{\partial r}$ is given by $\frac{\partial K^*}{\partial c} \frac{\partial c}{\partial r}$. Differentiating,

$$\frac{\partial K^*}{\partial c} = -\alpha \frac{pQ}{c^2} \quad \text{and} \quad \frac{\partial c}{\partial r} = q\left(\frac{1-uw}{1-u}\right),$$

therefore

$$\frac{\partial K^*}{\partial r} = \alpha \frac{pQ}{c^2} q\left(\frac{1-uw}{1-u}\right).$$

This can be calculated from an estimate of α and actual values of the variables p, Q, c, q, u and w. Since these values vary, it is necessary to choose a time on which to base the calculation. Jorgenson (1965, Table 2.8) calculates the effect of changes in market conditions (r, q, p) and tax parameters (u, v, w) using the values of the variables that held at the end of the sample period (fourth quarter, 1962). Jorgenson (1963, Table 3) presents long run responses ($\delta\frac{\partial K^*}{\partial r}$, etc.) using both average and end period values of the variables.

Likewise, elasticities can be obtained. However, this turns out to be uninteresting. Taking the simple case in which c is given as $q(\delta+r)$, we have

$$\frac{\partial K^*}{\partial q} = \frac{\partial K^*}{\partial c}\frac{\partial c}{\partial q} = -\alpha\frac{pQ}{c^2}(\delta+r),$$

so the elasticity with respect to q is

$$\frac{\partial \log K^*}{\partial \log q} = -\alpha\frac{pQ}{c^2}(\delta+r)\frac{q}{K^*} = -1.$$

The elasticity of capital stock with respect to the relative price ratio is also one, as is the elasticity with respect to output, which is easily seen by noting that in $K^* = \alpha(\frac{p}{c})Q$, the exponents of $\frac{p}{c}$ and Q are 1. These follow from the unit elasticity of substitution in the Cobb-Douglas production function, which is part of Jorgenson's maintained hypothesis - an assumption underlying his basic tests which is maintained and not itself tested. Jorgenson's work estimates the time shape of responses but these unitary elasticities are built into his model. Critics have suggested that this should be an open question, and to this we now turn.

Tests of Jorgenson's maintained hypotheses

As already observed, a noteworthy feature of Jorgenson's model is the explicit relation between investment demand and the underlying technology via the production function. Although a Cobb-Douglas production function is then assumed, other more general possibilities exist, and if the assumption that $\sigma = 1$ is relaxed then it is no longer the case that the elasticities with respect to relative prices and output are both equal to 1. Adopting a CES production function as an alternative,

$$Q = \gamma\{\delta K^{-\rho} + (1-\delta)L^{-\rho}\}^{-\nu/\rho}$$

the marginal productivity condition for capital is (cf. p.54)

$$K^{1+\rho} = \nu\delta\gamma^{-\rho/\nu} Q^{1+\rho/\nu} \frac{p}{c} .$$

Since $\sigma = \frac{1}{1+\rho}$, this gives as the equation for desired capital stock,

$$K^* = A(\frac{p}{c})^{\sigma} Q^{\sigma(1+\rho/\nu)} = A(\frac{p}{c})^{E_p} Q^{E_Q}, \text{ say,}$$

where E_p is the elasticity of desired (long run) K with respect to $\frac{p}{c}$ and E_Q is the elasticity with respect to output:

$$E_p = \sigma, \quad E_Q = \sigma + \frac{1-\sigma}{\nu} .$$

Only in the Cobb-Douglas case where $\sigma = 1$ is it necessarily true that $E_p = E_Q = 1$, although it is true that $E_Q = 1$ for any σ if there are constant returns to scale ($\nu = 1$). The combination $E_p = 0$ and $E_Q = 1$ takes us back to the simple accelerator.

Eisner and Nadiri (1968) point out that E_p and E_Q can be estimated in this more general specification, thus providing a test of Jorgenson's maintained hypothesis that both are equal to 1. Then one matter of interest is the effect of these alternative assumptions and estimates on the policy conclusions. The relation between net investment and changes in the determinants of K^* is estimated by Eisner and Nadiri in first-differenced logarithmic form:

$$\Delta\log K_t = \mu(L)\Delta\log K^*_t .$$

This form is convenient since the coefficients then give estimated elasticities directly, although the differences between the linear and log forms are small (Eisner and Nadiri, 1970). Taking the log of the above expression for K^*, the terms in relative prices and output enter separately, and using the rational lag function modified to permit these two determinants of K^* to have possibly different lag response functions, we have

$$\omega(L)\Delta\log K_t = \gamma_p(L)\Delta\log(\frac{p}{c}) + \gamma_Q(L)\Delta\log Q.$$

With the same specifications for ω and γ as used by Jorgenson and Stephenson, the estimating equation is

$$\Delta\log K_t = \sum_{i=n}^{k} \{\gamma_{pi}\,\Delta\log(\frac{p}{c})_{t-i} + \gamma_{Qi}\,\Delta\log Q_{t-i}\} - \omega_1\Delta\log K_{t-1} - \omega_2\Delta\log K_{t-2}\ .$$

(Eisner and Nadiri also question the Jorgenson - Stephenson restrictions on $\gamma(L)$, in which n is taken to be 3 or 4.)

There are two major consequences of this formulation. First, the long-run elasticities are estimated as

$$E_p = \frac{\Sigma\hat{\gamma}_{pi}}{1+\hat{\omega}_1+\hat{\omega}_2}, \qquad E_Q = \frac{\Sigma\hat{\gamma}_{Qi}}{1+\hat{\omega}_1+\hat{\omega}_2},$$

and not only are they not constrained to 1, they are also permitted to differ from each other. In this framework, Eisner and Nadiri first test whether the elasticities are the same, and then whether this common value is in fact 1. The simplest test of Jorgenson's maintained hypothesis that the elasticity with respect to $\frac{pQ}{c}$ is 1 is provided by setting $\gamma_{pi} = \gamma_{Qi}$ and estimating

$$\Delta\log K_t = \sum_{i=n}^{k} \gamma_i \log(\frac{pQ}{c})_{t-i} - \omega_1\Delta\log K_{t-1} - \omega_2\Delta\log K_{t-2}\ ,$$

then testing whether

$$\frac{\Sigma\hat{\gamma}_i}{1+\hat{\omega}_1+\hat{\omega}_2} = 1.$$

The second consequence is that having entered $\frac{p}{c}$ and Q with separate lag polynomials, we permit the time response of net investment to changes in either relative prices or output to differ, although Jorgenson's policy analyses assume the pattern of response of net investment is the same. The point is that net investment may well react with a different delay to an output change than it would to a change in the tax rate. Since the dynamic specification is rather ad hoc, and not itself supported by an economic model, it should not be subjected to needless restrictions in estimation.

Bischoff (1969) relaxes a further maintained hypothesis which relates to the specification of the error terms - the errors in the final estimating equation are assumed free of autocorrelation. (Eisner and Nadiri (1968), for comparability with Jorgenson, also assume independent errors.) Observe that adding an error term u_t to the exact equation $\Delta K_t = \mu(L)\Delta K^*_t$ produces a moving average error of the form $u_t + \omega_1 u_{t-1} + \omega_2 u_{t-2}$ in the final estimating equation, as noted above (p. 83). Similarly, if a multiplicative error u_t is added to the equation for K^* to represent the influence of omitted variables on the determination of desired capital stock, then the equation for $\Delta \log K_t$ has a disturbance term $\gamma(L)\log u_t$. These and other possibilities result in a suspicion of autocorrelated errors which, if correct, renders OLS estimates inconsistent. As a first approximation, Bischoff allows the error term w_t in the levels equation (rather than the first difference version)

$$\log K_t = \ldots - \omega_1 \log K_{t-1} - \omega_2 \log K_{t-2} + w_t$$

to be a first-order autoregression:

$$w_t = \rho w_{t-1} + \varepsilon_t .$$

Only if $\rho = 0$ are OLS estimates of the levels equation consistent; only if $\rho = 1$ does OLS estimation using first differences provide consistent estimates. Note that this assumption is only one stage better than the previous maintained hypothesis as it uses only a first-order autoregression. However, if the error is truly of this form, then the best estimates of the regression coefficients and ρ can be found by transforming the equation by $(1-\rho L)$, estimating for different values of ρ, $-1<\rho<1$, and choosing that value of ρ (and the corresponding regression coefficients) which minimise the residual sum of squares.

One practical problem lies in the difficulty of testing (or accurately estimating) the ratio estimates of elasticities given above (p. 92). In general, when estimating an equation whose coefficients are functions of the structural parameters, it is necessary to unscramble the regression coefficients to obtain structural parameter estimates. When this involves taking ratios of functions of regression coefficients where the denominator is quite small (in some cases $1+\hat{\omega}_1+\hat{\omega}_2$ is close to zero), the operation is fairly tricky - a small discrepancy due to sampling errors in a relatively small denominator will have a substantial effect on the ratio. Thus we expect not to be able to estimate ratios of this kind very accurately. The empirical results yield estimated elasticities which have high standard errors, and this can largely be attributed to the expression in the denominator being small and itself subject to error.

After much argument*, which need not be repeated here, the estimated price elasticity appears to be significantly below 1 (of the order of 0.1 - 0.2), contrary to Jorgenson's maintained hypothesis, and the overall role of relative prices is rather slight. The estimated elasticity with respect to output also tends to be below 1, though the departures from 1 are not so significant. Lastly the lag distributions with respect to price and output effects do appear to differ, with the response to relative price changes being rather slower than the response to output changes. However, all these estimates are derived from equations in which output is treated as exogenous, and we finally consider the effect of this specification error.

Endogeneity and dynamics

As we have seen, the approach adopted by Jorgenson and his forerunners separates the calculation of the firm's desired capital stock K^* from the determination of investment expenditures over time. In Jorgenson's case, the value of K^* results from a profit maximisation

* Eisner and Nadiri (1968, 1970), Bischoff (1969), and Jorgenson and Stephenson (1969b).

calculation, and this is then translated into an investment path by unforeseen delivery lags. The assumption that delivery delays continue to surprise the firm seems rather unlikely, for having regularly observed that orders for new machinery are not fulfilled instantaneously, a sensible manager will begin to take this fact into account. More generally, as Gould (1969) points out, the firm will recognise the interactions between the calculation of K^* and the adjustment process, possibly regarding the latter as a constraint in profit maximization. Thus the optimal behaviour in the static model will not be optimal in a dynamic world.

To illustrate this interaction in the context of Jorgenson's model, assume that the exogenous variables (interest rate, prices and so forth) have remained constant for some time, so that the firm has adjusted to its equilibrium capital stock position. Output and input levels are Q_0, K_0, and L_0, say, as given by the solution of the marginal productivity conditions and the production function, and investment expenditure is incurred only for the replacement of worn-out machines, at a constant rate. Now suppose that the interest rate falls to a new value r_1, which the firm expects to hold for some time. The long-run equilibrium or comparative static solution is given by the values Q_1, K_1, and L_1, obtained in terms of the exogenous variable values by solving the three equations as before. Since there are no adjustment costs, the optimal strategy for the firm is to get to this new position as quickly as possible, and orders should be immediately placed to increase capital stock from K_0 to K_1. Investment expenditure for expansion of capacity, IE, then takes the values $\mu_j(K_1-K_0)$, $j=0,1,\ldots$, over the next few periods. During this interregnum, the capital stock is constrained by the rate at which new machines can be delivered, and the firm chooses the optimal values of Q and L, given K. However, in the Jorgenson model, the firm first solves the labour marginal productivity condition and the production function for Q and L, given the existing capital stock, and then uses this value of Q to calculate K^*. At the new interest rate r_1, the values of Q and L calculated in terms of K_0 will be below the equilibrium values Q_1 and L_1, hence the resulting K^* value will be below K_1, and a sub-optimal quantity of investment projects will be initiated. Thus the adjustment to the new equilibrium position is rather slower than is optimal. Indeed, if there are no deliveries of new machines until two periods have elapsed, as in Jorgenson's empirical work, then the second round of adjustment will not occur until then, for the capital stock remains at K_0, and Q and L remain at the values given by K_0 and r_1, hence K^* does not change, and no further orders are placed to move towards K_1 until the capital stock changes from K_0 when the first new delivery arrives.

The conclusion is that the investment path given by the Jorgenson approach is not consistent with profit-maximising behaviour. In this dynamic framework, output is an inappropriate determinant of desired capital stock and hence investment, for it is itself an endogenous variable. Note that this criticism is independent of the particular production function adopted, and applies equally to the work of Eisner and Nadiri. What is required is an expression for K^* entirely in terms of exogenous variables, in order that a genuine reduced form equation can be derived, which might then facilitate links with the remainder of the economy.

As a final point of interest, we can ask how such an equation would be interpreted in the Jorgenson context, in particular with respect to the coefficient α. The reduced form expression for K for a profit-maximising perfectly competitive Cobb-Douglas ($\alpha+\beta<1$) firm is given by the solution of the three-equation system on p.35, which in the notation of this chapter is as follows:

$$K = (A\alpha^{1-\beta}\beta^{\beta}pc^{-(1-\beta)}\quad s^{-\beta})^{1/1-\alpha-\beta} \quad .$$

In the present situation, this equation determines K^*, before delivery lags set in. The corresponding Jorgenson equation is $K^* = \alpha(pQ/c)$. In either case, an investment equation is obtained by imposing a lag function $\mu(L)$, although this is not our main concern. However it might overcome the problem of simultaneity, for if Q only appears in the investment function with a lag of at least two periods, then it can be treated as a predetermined variable under appropriate assumptions about the error term. If firms were behaving optimally, but an investigator thought that they were obeying the Jorgenson K^* relation, then the estimated equation would be mis-specified, erroneously including Q and excluding s, and imposing unwarranted restrictions on the coefficients. It is difficult to say what are the effects of such specification errors, but even if they were zero, the interpretation of the constant term or scale factor is erroneous. The scale factor which the investigator would interpret as an estimate of α is really an estimate of $(A\alpha^{1-\beta}\ \beta^{\beta})^{1/1-\alpha-\beta}$. If Q is measured in appropriate units so that A=1, then for $\alpha+\beta$ not too far below 1 this scale factor is a very small number (.004 if $\alpha = 0.3$, $\beta = 0.6$), and if A is not equal to 1, or specification errors have an influence, then the scale factor will be a mixture of these various effects, and almost certainly not equal to α. Thus the reason why one would not wish to estimate the parameters of production functions from Jorgenson's theory of investment behaviour is that they would be subject to specification error.

Postscript

Recent items of note are the estimation of an Eisner-Nadiri equation from U.K. data by Boatwright and Eaton (1972) and the discussion of the problems of formulating econometrically relevant dynamic theories with particular reference to investment behaviour by Nerlove (1972).

Chapter 4

SIMULTANEOUS EQUATION SYSTEMS

Introduction

In the preceding chapters, we have considered from time to time the problems which arise when it is explicitly acknowledged that the particular behavioural relationship under consideration is embedded in a system of equations describing the simultaneous interactions of the relevant variables. Thus we considered the consequences for estimates of the consumption function of the fact that income is not an exogenous variable but is jointly determined with consumption in a more extensive system of equations. Likewise, the theory of the firm was brought to bear on the production and investment decisions by postulating a perfectly competitive firm simultaneously deciding its output and input levels, and subsequently its demand for capital goods, in the face of given prices, wages, and interest rates. Nevertheless attention remained concentrated on the particular behavioural relationship itself, and the model constructed around it was often relatively simple. Other components of income were not considered at the same time as consumption, nor was the determination of prices, wages, and interest rates considered along with production and investment.

We now discuss more complete simultaneous equation systems. In *Introductory Econometrics*, our examples were demand and supply models and national income determination systems, and so it is here. We first consider an example of a complete model of an individual market, and then discuss the construction and use of macroeconometric models.

A demand and supply model: the U.S. watermelon market

The study of the watermelon market by Suits (1955) was one of the first in which both demand and supply schedules were estimated for the same market, and it also provided an interesting twist to the cobweb model. Subsequently the model was reformulated as a causal chain by Wold (1958), and subjected to forecasting tests by l'Esperance (1964).

The first equation is a crop supply schedule, which essentially describes planting decisions, and relates the total number of watermelons available for harvest Q, to various prices in the previous season. These are the "own" price of watermelons P, and the prices of two commodities competing for farm space: cotton (C) and other vegetables (T). The estimated equation is

$$Q = \underset{(.156)}{0.587}\, P_{-1} - \underset{(.095)}{0.320}\, C_{-1} - \underset{(.238)}{0.141}\, T_{-1} \qquad (1)$$

(the subscript -1 indicates a one-period lagged value). All equations are fitted using logarithms of the variables, so that the coefficients are estimated elasticities, thus the price elasticity of crop supply is about 0.6. For convenience the intercept term is not reported here, nor are the coefficients of dummy variables relating to World War II and government cotton policy.

While the crop supply given by this equation is the quantity of watermelons available for harvest, the actual harvesting decision is influenced by current prices - if there is an insufficient margin, the crop is left unharvested. The number of watermelons harvested X, cannot of course exceed the crop Q, but is otherwise determined by the current price measured relative to the farm wage rate W, thus

$$X = \underset{(.110)}{0.237}\, P/W + \underset{(.114)}{1.205}\, Q \qquad \text{or} \qquad (2a)$$

$$X = Q \qquad (2b)$$

whichever is smaller. The first alternative is estimated by ignoring all years in which no unharvested crop is reported. The price elasticity of harvested supply is considerably smaller than that of crop supply, as might be expected, and the proportion of the crop harvested increases as the crop increases; note however that the coefficient of Q is not significantly different from 1.

The demand equation relates the current (farm) price to per capita disposable income Y/N, and per capita market supply X/N, together with an index of freight costs F:

$$P = \underset{(.088)}{1.530}\ Y/N - \underset{(.246)}{1.110}\ X/N - \underset{(.183)}{0.682}\ F. \qquad (3)$$

Rewriting this equation with demand, X/N, on the left hand side yields a derived estimate of the price elasticity of demand of $-1/1.110 = -0.9$, and an estimated income elasticity of $1.530/1.110 = 1.4$.

The endogenous variables are Q, X, and P; the justification for treating Y and W as exogenous is that the watermelon market not only represents a very small share of national income but also has a relative small influence, via the demand for labour, on farm wages. The first equation was estimated by OLS, as all the explanatory variables are predetermined, using data for the years 1919-1951. The remaining two equations contain endogenous variables on the right hand side, and so were estimated by limited information maximum likelihood, a method applicable to overidentified simultaneous equations taken one at a time, (and asymptotically equivalent to 2SLS). Observations on X were not available in the early part of the sample period, so these equations were estimated for 1930-1951.

The dynamic structure of the model is different from that of the simple cobweb model, in which price and quantity are sequentially determined. Instead, the previous value of P determines the current value of production Q, which in turn gives a kinked harvest supply schedule, and this in conjunction with the demand schedule gives the quantity sold X and the new price. Nevertheless, a final equation for P can be obtained as usual. On eliminating X and Q from equations (1), (2a), and (3) we obtain a final equation relating current price to its lagged value and a function of other exogenous variables, H say, as follows:

$$P_t = -0.622\,P_{t-1} + H_t.$$

If the values of the variables are such that (2b) is relevant, then the final equation becomes

$$P_t = -0.652\,P_{t-1} + H^*_t.$$

Whether one equation or the other or some mixture of the two provides a description of the behaviour of prices over time, the system clearly is stable, approaching equilibrium in an oscillatory fashion. It is difficult to think of a situation in which a proportion of the crop is persistently left unharvested as an equilibrium position, although it could easily arise in the present formulation as a result of high wage rates. One might imagine that in a genuine equilibrium situation farmers would take such factors into account and ensure that the complete crop was harvested, which suggests that in the general situation the lagged wage rate might appear as a further explanatory variable in equation (1).

Wold (1958) reformulated the model as a causal chain or recursive system (cf. *IE*, §5.8). The supply relation remains as Suits' equation (1), already a single causal relation. The remaining equations are reformulated to provide descriptions of the behaviour of the separate economic agents: consumers who determine the level of demand, and merchants who regulate the price. Suppliers, consumers, and merchants are held to be autonomous, "in the sense that changes in the behaviour of one group do not necessarily bring about a change in the behaviour pattern of the other groups", that is, no feedback and uncorrelated disturbance terms. Then the equations can be estimated by OLS.

Consumer demand is denoted by X^*, given by the harvest X when only part of the crop is harvested, but unknown in the six years when $X = Q$. A general cost of living index, PI, is introduced, so that the per capita demand is determined by the relative price of watermelons and real per capita income*:

* Standard errors are not reported by Wold, and all the values given here result from my computations, using his data. There are small differences in the third decimal place of our coefficient values.

$$\frac{X^*}{N} = -\underset{(.148)}{0.205}\frac{P}{PI} + \underset{(.209)}{0.429}\frac{Y}{N.PI} \qquad (2')$$

The price mechanism is influenced by the difference between demand and supply, and real per capita income:

$$\frac{P}{PI} = \underset{(.420)}{0.266}\left[\left(\frac{X^*}{N}\right)_{-1} - \frac{Q}{N}\right] + \underset{(.163)}{1.216}\frac{Y}{N.PI} \qquad (3')$$

The one-year lag on X^*/N results from the argument that in fixing the current price, merchants have in mind expected or anticipated demand and supply, and whereas Q will be known as planting has already taken place, demand is expected to continue at the level of the preceding year; this seems to provide another example of ad hoc dynamics. Real income is included on the grounds that with increasing income, "there is more room for margins between price and production cost", and as an indicator of merchants' salary expenses.

The causal ordering is Q, P, X^*. However it is seen that once attention is paid to standard errors, the general specification is not well supported by the data. Otherwise, the second requirement for a recursive system, namely independent errors, although not examined by Wold does seem to be supported by equations (2') and (3') in particular, for the coefficient of correlation between the residuals of these two equations has a t-ratio of -1.18.

Various ex-post forecasting exercises were conducted with these models by l'Esperance (1964). It was first shown that Suits' solved structural form provided better forecasts than a directly estimated reduced form - no doubt the prior restrictions were of value, giving useful information (cf. *IE*, p. 111). Secondly, Suits' interdependent system did better than Wold's recursive version of the model, suggesting that the specification of the interdependent system is a better approximation in this case. Now that we have looked rather more closely at the lack of support for Wold's hypotheses offered by the data, this last finding is not surprising.

Macroeconometric models

We concentrate on the general principles of the construction and use of large-scale economy-wide models, and leave aside the detailed specifications of particular models, for there is little to be gained by singling out a current model and repeating at what would be considerable length the details of its equations, coefficients, and so forth. The one exception to this rule is a six-equation example discussed shortly, which also suggests that the cost of presenting the details of a much larger-scale model outweighs the benefits. The construction of many macroeconometric models is based on Keynesian theory and its developments, and the main uses are policy analysis and the examination of the behaviour of the system as a whole.

Nerlove (1966) describes, in summary form, the features of twenty-five statistical macro models, covering nine countries and ranging from the early models of Tinbergen (1939, 1951) and Klein (1950) to the massive Brookings-SSRC model of the U.S. economy (Duesenberry et al, 1965, 1969). American work predominates in this field, as does the name of Klein, but there are two current U.K. programmes of note. The only operational large-scale forecasting model is that of the London Business School*, developed by Professor Ball and his co-workers from the original quarterly U.K. model of Klein, Ball, Hazelwood, and Vandome (1961); forecasts from the LBS model are presented quarterly in the *Sunday Times*. Work on the development of a large model is in progress at Southampton University, and the general research strategy and results for certain sectors are described in various papers in Hilton and Heathfield (1970), which also reports a great deal of other applied econometric work on the U.K. economy.

The simple Keynesian model is in itself of little use for empirical work, but substantially developed (often in non-Keynesian ways) lies at the heart of most macroeconometric models. The elementary system represents the markets for goods, money, and labour. The goods market comprises a consumption function, an investment function, and an identity:

$$c = c(y), \quad i = i(r), \quad y = c + i,$$

* See, for example, the description of the model presented in Renton (1973), along with other macroeconometric studies.

(the identity having been obtained by eliminating savings, s, from $y = c + s$ and $s = i$). From this follows the IS curve as a partial reduced form relating income to the rate of interest. A further relation (the LM curve) can be derived from the liquidity preference function

$$M/p = ky + M_2(r),$$

assuming that the money supply M is exogenously given and equilibrium prevails. The IS and LM curves intersect at some combination of the interest rate and income, determining r and y assuming that the price level p is given. The labour market contains a production function giving real output as a function of employment n, a marginal productivity condition giving labour demand as a function of the real wage W/p, and a labour supply function in terms of the money wage:

$$y = y(n), \quad W/p = y'(n), \quad W = W_0 + W(n).$$

The whole system has seven equations, and determines the endogenous variables c, i, y, r, p, n, and W in terms of the exogenous variable M. Most of the basic relations have empirical counterparts in most macroeconometric models, although an exception is the labour supply function - labour supply is often regarded as demographically determined, without money illusion, and attention is concentrated on the determination of the level or rate of change of wages. However, a number of extensions are required to make the model useful for empirical work.

First, as it stands the model is entirely static and contains no dynamic behaviour, nor any link between one period and the next. The time period is assumed sufficiently short for capital stock to be taken as given, and the production function has a single argument, labour input. At the simplest level a link between periods could be obtained by letting investment accumulate and entering the resulting capital stock in the production function, and an immediate next step is an accelerator mechanism. It is necessary to introduce dynamic considerations for macroeconomic policy questions, where one is interested in short-run changes. The change in any single period will tend to be substantially less than the gross effect predicted by a static model, and the rate of approach to that long run position will be of interest. While longer term growth models are oriented towards the study of the behaviour of equilibrium growth paths, in short term models adjustments to disequilibrium positions, lag structures, and so forth are a major concern.

Secondly, further sectors are required, especially government and foreign trade sectors. For example, tax and government expenditure functions might be added, implicitly recognising a role for a financial sector and in a particular a supply of money function. Then the analysis of fiscal and monetary policy measures could be undertaken, and these might as a further development be treated endogenously themselves. Of course, in U.S. models the foreign sector is relatively smaller than is required in U.K. models.

Thirdly, disaggregation of the simple Keynesian model is required in various ways. With respect to the aggregate variables, the consumption of durables and non-durables plus services might be considered separately, for the speeds of adjustment and determinants of each component may be substantially different. Similarly investment may be broken down into expenditures on residential construction, plant and equipment, and inventories (stocks). Disaggregation of the income variable arises in a variety of ways since there is no unique definition of income in national accounts. Economic statisticians have been preoccupied to reconcile the three alternative GDP definitions - income, output and expenditure - or provide some compromise series. The income approach distinguishes wages and salaries, profits, and dividends. In the output approach value added is calculated by industry, which provides a further direction of disaggregation. The expenditure approach ($Y=C+I+G+X-M$) is implicit in the preceding remarks about additional sectors. Disaggregation over time has led from the early annual models of Tinbergen and Klein to the present-day quarterly models. These give a finer description of lag structures and are more useful in analyzing and forecasting business cycle developments. Quarterly models were constructed as soon as the requisite national income data became available, an important step being the quarterly model of the U.K. economy constructed by Klein et al (1961).

In developing the simple macro-model, one guide is provided by economic theory, as we have seen in the discussion of the specification of particular relationships in the preceding chapters. On the other hand, the problem to be solved influences the form of the model. Conventionally we distinguish between short and long run models: if we were interested in the gross (long run) outcome of economic changes, an annual model might suffice, whereas short-term policy analysis requires a quarterly model. The type of policy objective also influences the level of disaggregation and size of the model. To forecast GNP, for instance, a very disaggregated model might not be required: at one extreme a naive equation regressing present on past values of GNP might be satisfactory much of the time. However, it would tend to miss turning points and the response to other changes, and it is precisely at such times that guidance from a model is sought. So whether a large or small model is required depends on what it is for. A small model may successfully predict GNP but have nothing to say about the finer points of demand management. For this reason it may be a poor criticism that the larger model predicts total GNP less well than the smaller one - it may predict the components of GNP satisfactorily when the small model has nothing whatever to say about them. In both design and assessment of models the purpose served is fundamental. However, it is difficult to develop a method of appraising alternative models which serve different ends. What is lacking is some measure of the information value of larger size - the usefulness of disaggregation. Perhaps we need an experiment in which the outcomes of a "finely tuned" policy based on a large model are compared with the results of a simple aggregate "across-the-board" policy based on a small model (assuming that a measure of the outcomes can be agreed on).

In the construction of large-scale economy-wide models, an alternative approach is provided by the Cambridge model or "Programme for Growth"*. It is not concerned with short-term forecasting or policy analysis but yields projections under specific assumptions which attempt to show what the economy could look like ten or twenty years hence. The main departure from the statistical macroeconometric models discussed elsewhere in this chapter is that the relative

* See the papers published by Cambridge University, Department of Applied Economics, in the Programme for Growth series, under the general editorship of Stone.

emphasis on identities and behavioural relationships is precisely reversed. The identities hold the centre of the stage and are set out in a social accounting matrix with a considerable degree of disaggregation. In a recent version some 253 separate accounts have been identified, and checking the consistency of possible future values of some variables with other components of the accounts is a major task. The behavioural relationships used are generally of a rather simple kind, and are mainly concerned with the projection of components of final demand. This approach leads to input-output and activity analysis models, and is perhaps the more relevant form of economy-wide model for use in development economics.

Dynamic multipliers and policy analysis

The use of an estimated structural form in both ex-ante and ex-post forecasting exercises has already been discussed (*IE*, §5.10). From the estimated structural form of G linear equations

$$\hat{\mathbf{B}}\mathbf{y}_t + \hat{\mathbf{\Gamma}}\mathbf{z}_t = \mathbf{u}_t$$

the reduced form coefficients are estimated as

$$\hat{\mathbf{\Pi}} = -\hat{\mathbf{B}}^{-1}\hat{\mathbf{\Gamma}},$$

and the forecasting equations are of the form

$$\mathbf{y}_t = \hat{\mathbf{\Pi}}\mathbf{z}_t.$$

In this section we consider the dynamic properties of a model which contains lagged endogenous variables, and the simplest case arises when no variable occurs with more than a one-period lag (a generalisation is provided in the appendix to this chapter). Whether we are working with estimated coefficients, assumed values, or algebraic representations is of little consequence for the analysis, so we simplify by dropping hats, and also leave the error term aside. The reduced form equation then can be written

$$\mathbf{y}_t = \Pi_1 \mathbf{y}_{t-1} + \Pi_2 \mathbf{x}_t ,$$

where the vector of $(G+K)$ predetermined variables $\mathbf{z}_t$ has been partitioned into sub-vectors of G lagged endogenous variables $\mathbf{y}_{t-1}$ and K truly exogenous variables $\mathbf{x}_t$, and the Π matrix is conformably partitioned. Π_1 is of dimension $G \times G$, and if some particular endogenous variable does not appear lagged in any equation, then the corresponding column of Π_1 is zero.

The coefficients in the matrix Π_2 give the immediate change in the endogenous variables in response to a unit change in an exogenous variable - the impact multipliers. Subsequently a maintained change or step in an exogenous variable beginning at time t has continuing effects which work through the system as follows:

$$\mathbf{y}_t = \Pi_1 \mathbf{y}_{t-1} + \Pi_2 \mathbf{x}_t$$

$$\mathbf{y}_{t+1} = \Pi_1 \mathbf{y}_t + \Pi_2 \mathbf{x}_{t+1} = \Pi_1^2 \mathbf{y}_{t-1} + \Pi_1 \Pi_2 \mathbf{x}_t + \Pi_2 \mathbf{x}_{t+1}$$

$$\mathbf{y}_{t+2} = \Pi_1 \mathbf{y}_{t+1} + \Pi_2 \mathbf{x}_{t+2} = \Pi_1^3 \mathbf{y}_{t-1} + \Pi_1^2 \Pi_2 \mathbf{x}_t + \Pi_1 \Pi_2 \mathbf{x}_{t+1} + \Pi_2 \mathbf{x}_{t+2}$$

and so on. Thus, whereas the impact multipliers are given by Π_2, the various dynamic multipliers are given by

$\Pi_2 + \Pi_1 \Pi_2$	for the effect after one period
$(I + \Pi_1 + \Pi_1^2)\Pi_2$	for the effect after two periods
$\vdots$	$\vdots$
$(I + \Pi_1 + \ldots + \Pi_1^j)\Pi_2$	for the effect after j periods.

If the matrix Π_1 is such that Π_1^j tends to a zero matrix as $j \to \infty$, then the total or long-run effect is given by

$$\sum_{j=0}^{\infty} \Pi_1^j \Pi_2 = (I - \Pi_1)^{-1} \Pi_2 .$$

These quantities are called equilibrium multipliers by Goldberger (1959); the (g,k) element describes the change in the equilibrium or long-run level of the endogenous variable y_g in response to a unit change in the exogenous variable x_k. The condition for Π_1^j to converge to zero as j increases is that all the eigenvalues of the matrix Π_1 have modulus less than 1, and this provides a stability condition for the model (cf. Glaister, 1972, Ch. 9). The nature of these eigenvalues determines the speed of approach to equilibrium, and whether this approach is smooth or oscillatory. In practice, the corresponding eigenvalues calculated from estimated coefficients provide useful information about the adequacy of the dynamic specification of the model; in particular, if a calculated eigenvalue is substantially greater than 1 while the underlying actual situation is essentially stable, the estimated model cannot be accepted as a realistic representation.

The effects over time of an exogenous variable used as a policy instrument are given by these dynamic multipliers. Since we have a linear model, the effect of a policy package can be evaluated by combining the appropriate dynamic or equilibrium multipliers. Suits (1962, §1) presents some simple examples in the context of an illustrative four-equation model. For instance, an increase in government spending is combined with an increase in the tax schedule (via its intercept term). Such a policy package may be described as an ex-ante balanced budget policy, for both government income and expenditure are increased by the same amount, and corresponding balanced budget multipliers can be calculated. Ex-post, however, the policy yields a surplus, for while the increase in government expenditure is balanced by the increased tax yield at the original level of income, the policy itself changes income and hence the tax yield, which no longer exactly balances the budget. Since the effect of government expenditure on income is greater than that of taxation, income and hence the tax yield increase, giving an ex-post budget surplus in this example.

An illustration: Klein Model I

As an example of an estimated model, we present the six-equation Keynesian income-expenditure model of the U.S. economy, 1921-1941, by Klein (1950), known as Klein's Model I. Although very much on the small side by current standards, it will serve to illustrate the analysis without obscuring it in a more detailed specification.

Over the years, the model has also been used as a test-bed for virtually every new technique of estimation and analysis that has been introduced.

The consumption function allows differing propensities to consume for different components or classes of income, so aggregate consumption (C) is a function of profits (P) current and lagged, and the sum of the wage bill in private industry (W_1) and government (W_2):

$$C = 16.79 + 0.020\,P + 0.235\,P_{-1} + 0.800\,(W_1 + W_2) + \hat{u}_1 .$$

A profits theory of investment is adopted, so net investment (I) is given in terms of current and lagged profits, and beginning-year capital stock (K_{-1}):

$$I = 17.78 + 0.231\,P + 0.546\,P_{-1} - 0.146\,K_{-1} + \hat{u}_2 .$$

A labour demand equation follows, giving the private wage bill as a function of net national income (Y) plus business taxes (T) less the government wage bill, all current and lagged, together with a time trend (measured in calendar years):

$$W_1 = 1.60 + 0.420\,(Y+T-W_2) + 0.164\,(Y+T-W_2)_{-1} + 0.135\,(t-1935) + \hat{u}_3 .$$

Then follow three identities, namely the expenditure and income definitions of national income, and the definition of net investment:

$$\begin{aligned} Y + T &= C + I + G \\ Y &= W_1 + W_2 + P \\ I &= K - K_{-1} . \end{aligned}$$

The endogenous variables are C, I, W_1, Y, P, and K, and there are four exogenous variables: W_2, T, G, and t. Adding lagged variables, the total number of predetermined variables appearing in the model is nine. Thus each of the first three equations is over-identified, and the estimates reported above are obtained by the method of full-information maximum likelihood, which estimates the whole model simultaneously, taking all the restrictions into account.

In presenting the reduced form, we re-order the endogenous variables so that the zero columns of the matrix Π_1, corresponding to variables whose lagged values do not appear, are the last three columns. The reduced form coefficients, given by Theil and Boot (1962), are as follows:

$$\begin{pmatrix} P \\ Y \\ K \\ C \\ W_1 \\ I \end{pmatrix} = \begin{pmatrix} 0.863 & -0.063 & -0.164 & 0 & 0 & 0 \\ 1.489 & 0.174 & -0.283 & 0 & 0 & 0 \\ 0.746 & -0.015 & 0.816 & 0 & 0 & 0 \\ 0.743 & 0.189 & -0.098 & 0 & 0 & 0 \\ 0.626 & 0.237 & -0.119 & 0 & 0 & 0 \\ 0.746 & -0.015 & -0.184 & 0 & 0 & 0 \end{pmatrix} \begin{pmatrix} P \\ Y \\ K \\ C \\ W_1 \\ I \end{pmatrix}_{-1}$$

$$+ \begin{pmatrix} -0.224 & -1.281 & 1.119 & -0.052 & 0.063 & -0.063 \\ 0.614 & -1.484 & 1.930 & 0.143 & -0.174 & 0.174 \\ -0.052 & -0.296 & 0.259 & -0.012 & 0.015 & -0.015 \\ 0.666 & -0.188 & 0.671 & 0.155 & -0.189 & 0.189 \\ -0.162 & -0.204 & 0.811 & 0.195 & -0.237 & 0.237 \\ -0.052 & -0.296 & 0.259 & -0.012 & 0.015 & -0.015 \end{pmatrix} \begin{pmatrix} W_2 \\ T \\ G \\ t \\ (W_2)_{-1} \\ T_{-1} \end{pmatrix}$$

Thus a billion dollar increase in government expenditure increases consumption in the current period by 0.671 billions, and the ex-ante balanced budget income multiplier is 1.930 - 1.484 = 0.446. Theil and Boot go on to calculate elements of the matrices $\Pi_1^j \Pi_2$, or "interim multipliers", which give the effect of a unit shock (not sustained) in an exogenous variable on an endogenous variable j periods later. Changes in sign occur, for the system oscillates as it returns to equilibrium. (Note that some care is needed in the treatment of lagged exogenous variables in these calculations. Note also that the term "final equation", which following Tinbergen (1939) we have used to denote an equation relating on endogenous variable to its own lagged values and exogenous variables, is used by Theil and Boot for the solution of this equation, that is, an expression for a current endogenous variable in terms of the infinite past of the exogenous variables.) Total multipliers of the form $\sum_{j=0}^{\infty} \Pi_1^j \Pi_2 = (I-\Pi_1)^{-1} \Pi_2$ are also presented for maintained changes in three of the exogenous variables as follows:

	P	Y	K	C	W_1	I
W_2	-0.192	0.536	-1.024	0.536	-0.271	0
T	-1.237	-1.569	-6.564	-0.569	-0.333	0
G	0.965	2.323	5.123	1.323	1.358	0

Thus the ex-ante balanced budget income multiplier in the long run is 2.323 - 1.569 = 0.754, and so about three-fifths of the long run effect occurs in the first year.

Finally, the question of stability can be investigated by calculating the eigenvalues of Π_1. Of course, having already observed that the interim multipliers die away as j increases, we expect to find that the eigenvalues have modulus less than 1. Since Π_1 has three zero columns, there are only three non-zero eigenvalues, and these are obtained as the eigenvalues of the 3×3 submatrix in the top left-hand corner. The latent roots given by Theil and Boot comprise one real root and a pair of complex conjugate roots:

$$\lambda_1, \lambda_2 = 0.838 (\cos 0.435 \pm i \sin 0.435)$$

$$\lambda_3 = 0.334.$$

Clearly, these roots have modulus less than 1, so the system is stable though oscillatory.

Stochastic simulation

The preceding discussion has dealt with exact models, and the fact that each behavioural equation contains a random error term has been ignored. Of course in forecasting exercises, even though the presence of the disturbance term is acknowledged, the usual course of action is to set it equal to its expected value of zero, in the absence of other information about its likely value. The dynamic properties of inexact models have been explored by stochastic simulation methods, in which artificially generated random numbers are added to the estimated equations. This is not intended to improve the forecasts, but simply to see whether the behaviour of the endogenous variables as given by the model acknowledging the presence of random variation approximates the behaviour of the actual series. Thus further information about the dynamics of the model and the accuracy of its representation of the real world is obtained.

Adelman and Adelman (1959) investigated the dynamic properties of the 25-equation U.S. annual model of Klein and Goldberger (1955) in this way. (A linearized version of the model was used, to avoid problems discussed in the next section.) Having added disturbance terms to the estimated structural equations, the solution of the system gives each endogenous variable in terms of predetermined variables and error terms. By assuming that the exogenous variables follow linear trends, and using computer generated random values of the error terms (with variances equal to the sample-period residual variances), values of the endogenous variables are obtained. The Adelmans found that the generated paths of the endogenous variables exhibited cyclical fluctuations about linear trends. Their answer to the question of how to assess the correspondence between the behaviour of the simulated values and the actual series was to apply the National Bureau of Economic Research business cycle methodology to the simulated series. In terms of the length of cycles, the coincidence of turning points of various series, and the lead-lag relationship of various series to the reference cycle, the simulated fluctuations were "remarkably similar to those described by the NBER as characterizing the United States economy." Thus they concluded that the Klein-Goldberger model, with the presence of random errors acknowledged, provided a useful approximation to the U.S. economy*.

Random errors in the equations were the Adelmans' "shocks of Type II", they also investigated the effect of "shocks of Type I", namely random errors added to the linear projections of the exogenous variables, so that these behaved more like observed series. In practice there was little improvement in realism using shocks of Type I, for the predicted endogenous variables still had very smooth trends, without the sort of cyclical behaviour observed in the actual economy.

* Studies contained in Hickman (1972) report similar findings for more recent large U.S. quarterly models, with one modification. When the simulated error terms are intercorrelated and autocorrelated to the extent that the sample period residuals are, the cyclical correspondence is improved.

The problem of non-linearity

As well as ignoring disturbance terms, the earlier discussion assumed that we were working with linear models, whereas most macro-models have some non-linearity in variables. Non-linear relationships can sometimes be transformed to give a linear-in-parameters equation, but this typically produces non-linearities in variables, for example, the logarithmic transformation of a Cobb-Douglas production function. Further possibilities arise from the occurrence of products or ratios of variables which also appear separately, e.g. the wage bill equals the wage rate times the number employed, and the unemployment rate equals the number employed divided by the total labour force. The presence of price variables typically requires products or ratios of variables if real variables are used in some sectors and monetary variables in others, and relative prices may enter demand functions.

Estimation problems can be overcome so long as the equations are linear in the parameters, assuming that such methods as 2SLS, which treat the structural equations one at a time, are employed. The problem of non-linearity arises at the solution or forecasting stage, because there is no longer a simple reduced form expression available. Some variables may appear, in one form or another, in more than one place in the vector of endogenous variables; for example, variables of the form y_i/y_j, $y_i y_k$, and $\log y_k$ may appear in addition to the basic variables y_i, y_j, y_k. Thus the y-vector contains more elements than the number of basic endogenous variables (and equations), and a general linear reduced form expression for the basic endogenous variables does not exist. If we attempted to treat the additional non-linear variables as separate variables, adding identities such as $y^\dagger = y_i/y_j$, the reduced form expressions will not in general be internally consistent. For example, given exogenous variable values, the reduced form prediction for y_i divided by the reduced form prediction for y_j will not in general equal the reduced form prediction for $y^\dagger$. In this situation, solution of the system

$$\mathbf{B}\mathbf{y}_t + \mathbf{\Gamma}\mathbf{z}_t = \mathbf{0}$$

for the values of the basic endogenous variables contained within $\mathbf{y}_t$ proceeds by numerical methods. Given estimates of the coefficients and projected values for the z-variables, the computer seeks, by iterative methods, values for the endogenous variables which satisfy the above equation to the desired degree of accuracy. In practice we do not get exactly zero on the right hand side, but we instruct the computer to keep "improving" the solution values for the endogenous variables until the right hand side is less than some very small preassigned number.

The amount of computation required can be substantially reduced if the model can be set out in recursive blocks. In a recursive model the matrix of coefficients of the endogenous variables is triangular; in a block-recursive model, the matrix is block-triangular, and taking the case in which the model can be subdivided into three blocks as an illustration, the above equation can be written

$$\begin{pmatrix} \mathbf{B}^{11} & 0 & 0 \\ \mathbf{B}^{21} & \mathbf{B}^{22} & 0 \\ \mathbf{B}^{31} & \mathbf{B}^{32} & \mathbf{B}^{33} \end{pmatrix} \begin{pmatrix} \mathbf{y}_t^1 \\ \mathbf{y}_t^2 \\ \mathbf{y}_t^3 \end{pmatrix} + \Gamma \mathbf{z}_t = 0.$$

The diagonal blocks $\mathbf{B}^{jj}$ are square matrices, $G_j \times G_j$ say, and the sub-vectors $\mathbf{y}_t^j$ are G_j-component vectors, thus feedbacks within blocks are taken into account. Note that this structure is not being used as grounds for applying block-by-block or even OLS estimation methods, for each block could only be separately estimated if the errors in different blocks were mutually uncorrelated. It is assumed that the system has been estimated by some appropriate method, such as 2SLS, and the block-recursive structure is used simply to ease the computational burden in obtaining solutions for the endogenous variables in the presence of non-linearities. Solution begins by solving the first block of equations for $\mathbf{y}_t^1$ - there are no feedback relations from the second and third blocks, $\mathbf{y}_t^1$ being given in terms of estimated coefficients and predetermined variables. These solution values for the first block can then be regarded as predetermined when we come to solve for $\mathbf{y}_t^2$. Finally, solutions for the elements of $\mathbf{y}_t^3$ are obtained in terms of predetermined variables and the solution values of $\mathbf{y}_t^1$ and $\mathbf{y}_t^2$ - elements of $\mathbf{y}_t^3$ have no influence in the first two blocks. Thus one large problem becomes three small ones. In practice, seeing whether there is a suitable ordering of equations and endogenous variables so that a large model can be set out in this way is itself a non-trivial computer exercise, but one worth doing. The block-recursive structure is a feature of most recent large models.

A further problem in non-linear models is that the multiplier expressions derived earlier no longer apply, for there is no longer an explicit reduced form. This is illustrated by a simple example which distinguishes real and monetary variables.

$$C = \alpha + \beta Y$$

$$Y = C + I$$

$$p_c C + p_k I = pY \qquad \text{endogenous: } C, Y, p_c, p$$

$$p_c = \gamma + \delta p \qquad \text{exogenous: } I, p_k$$

The variables C, I, and Y are given in real terms, and the third equation is an identity which says that money income is given by multiplying C and I by price indices for consumption and capital goods. The fourth equation is a price behaviour equation giving the price index for consumption goods as a linear function of the overall index. The model breaks down into two blocks: the first two equations determine C and Y given I, and the last two equations then determine p and p_c in terms of C, Y, I, and p_k. The reduced form of the first block gives the basic multiplier in real (constant price) terms:

$$\frac{\Delta Y}{\Delta I} = \frac{1}{1-\beta},$$

and this is, as usual, entirely a function of the parameters of the model. But if we require multipliers in (current) money values and seek, for example, an expression giving the relationship between a change in money income (pY) and current autonomous expenditure ($p_k I$), then we can only obtain an expression which also involves the values of some variables. Substituting into the third equation from the fourth and first gives:

$$pY = (\gamma+\delta p)(\alpha+\beta Y) + p_k I.$$

Thus

$$(1-\beta\delta)pY = \alpha\delta p + \gamma\beta Y + p_k I + \alpha\gamma$$

and

$$(1-\beta\delta)\Delta(pY) = \alpha\delta\Delta p + \gamma\beta\Delta Y + \Delta(p_k I).$$

To get the current value multiplier $\Delta(pY)/\Delta(p_k I)$ we now need to eliminate Δp and ΔY. From the first block's reduced form we have

$$Y = \frac{\alpha+I}{1-\beta} = \frac{p_k(\alpha+I)}{p_k(1-\beta)}, \quad \text{and so} \quad \Delta Y = \frac{\Delta(p_k I)}{p_k(1-\beta)}.$$

Also by definition $\Delta(pY) = p\Delta Y + Y\Delta p - \Delta p\Delta y$, and neglecting $\Delta p\Delta y$ which is small compared with other terms gives

$$\Delta p = \frac{\Delta(pY)}{Y} - \frac{p}{Y}\Delta Y = \frac{\Delta(pY)}{Y} - \frac{p}{Y}\frac{\Delta(p_k I)}{p_k(1-\beta)}.$$

So substituting in for Δp and ΔY we have

$$(1-\beta\delta)\Delta(pY) = \alpha\delta\frac{\Delta(pY)}{Y} - \alpha\delta\frac{p}{Y}\frac{\Delta(p_k I)}{p_k(1-\beta)} + \gamma\beta\frac{\Delta(p_k I)}{p_k(1-\beta)} + \Delta(p_k I),$$

which finally yields the current value multiplier expressed in terms of parameter values and unfortunately, other variables as well:

$$\frac{\Delta(pY)}{\Delta(p_k I)} = \frac{1 - \frac{\alpha\delta p}{p_k Y(1-\beta)} + \frac{\gamma\beta}{p_k(1-\beta)}}{1 - \beta\delta - \alpha\delta/Y}.$$

If we assume equal prices so that $p = p_c = p_k$ (i.e. $\gamma = 0$, $\delta = 1$), then the current value multiplier collapses to the real multiplier:

$$\frac{\Delta(pY)}{\Delta(p_k I)} = \frac{1 - \dfrac{\alpha}{Y(1-\beta)}}{1 - \beta - \alpha/Y} = \frac{1}{1-\beta} = \frac{\Delta Y}{\Delta I} .$$

Otherwise multipliers depend on the levels of the variables at which they are calculated and are not simple functions of parameters of the system. Hence for policy analysis in non-linear models it is necessary to specify the actual values of variables appearing on the right hand side, and multipliers may be different at different states of the economy.

Even in a linear model, multiplier effects of a change in a parameter are equally difficult to analyse (which explains why Suits (1962) alters the intercept of his tax function rather than the tax rate): they also require non-linear solution methods

In this situation, multiplier analysis proceeds by non-stochastic simulation. Solutions for the endogenous variables over a number of periods are obtained by the methods discussed above, and the effect of a unit change in an exogenous variable is obtained by recomputing the solution with the changed value of that variable. If this exercise is done outside the sample period, with known values of the exogenous variables, then the sequence of ex-post forecasts $\mathbf{y}_{T+j}$, j = 1, 2, ... gives the "control solution". Let $\mathbf{y}^*_{T+j}$ be the disturbed solution obtained when a particular exogenous variable $x_{k,T+j}$ is replaced by $x_{k,T+j} + \delta$, j = 1, 2, ... The dynamic multipliers are then given as $(\mathbf{y}^*_{T+j} - \tilde{\mathbf{y}}_{T+j})/\delta$, j = 1, 2, ... Thus the multipliers, although obtained in a completely different way, still describe the changes in the endogenous variables over time in response to a unit change in an exogenous variable. Note that if the model is highly non-linear, these multipliers may vary with the size of the perturbation δ; however this does not seem to be a serious problem in practice.

This method is used by Evans (1969a) to calculate estimates of the balanced budget multipliers, using the Wharton quarterly econometric forecasting model, as described by Evans and Klein (1968). To give the flavour of the findings, if non-defence government spending is increased by $1 billion and personal taxes raised by the same amount to give an ex-ante balanced budget, the multiplier is 0.85 in the first quarter declining to 0.31 after 40 quarters. This generates a surplus since the increase in government expenditure itself generates an increase in tax revenues. If an ex-post balanced budget multiplier is required then following a $1 billion increase in government spending personal taxes must be adjusted each quarter by the amount necessary to balance the budget ex-post. This procedure yields multipliers of 1.72, 2.50, 1.91,...,1.23 (after 40 quarters). These latter values are higher, as one would expect, since the required increase in personal taxes is less than the $1 billion imposed in the ex-ante case.

Policy analysis proceeds in exactly the same way. Klein (1969) uses the Brookings model to analyse the effect of the 1964 tax cut. A control solution $\tilde{y}_{T+k}$ is calculated for the eight quarters 1963-64 using actual tax parameters, whose values changed at the beginning of 1964. A "status quo" solution is also calculated by keeping the tax parameters fixed at their 1963 levels throughout the 1964 calculations. The difference between the two solutions for the various endogenous variables of interest over the four quarters of 1964 then gives an estimate of the effect of the tax cut. Klein estimates that real GNP rose above its no-tax-cut value by $11.3 billion after four quarters, and that the unemployment rate was reduced by about 0.5 per cent.

Of course the multipliers elicit the properties of the model, whereas we are interested in the properties of the real economy. However, if the model has been shown to be a realistic representation of the economy in forecasting and other tests, one is justified in claiming some realism for subsequent multiplier analysis of policy alternatives. Hence forecasting tests are important validation exercises, even if one is not interested in forecasting per se. Such tests have already been discussed (*IE*, §5.10), attention having been paid to the difference between ex-ante and ex-post forecasts. The former correspond to the usual future prediction exercise where projections of exogenous variables have to be employed, but are not too helpful in comparing one model or forecasting group with another, for one group may simply be better at forecasting exogenous variables rather than model-building. It is also the practice in ex-ante forecasting to adjust the constant term in estimated equations to pull endogenous variables back on to the true path. This procedure is often justified in an ad hoc fashion, by arguing that some new institutional feature or data revision is affecting the model's performance in an unspecified or unestimable way. A theoretically more respectable argument in support of this procedure is that it is taking serial correlation in the error term into account. If the error term is independent, then the best that can be done is to estimate next period's disturbance at its expected value of zero. However, if $u_t = \rho u_{t-1} + \varepsilon_t$, and the current forecast error $\hat{u}_T$ is already known, then the best estimate of next period's disturbance is $\rho\hat{u}_T$, and this can be added into the equation, where it will appear as an adjustment to the constant term. In practice, ρ would not be known, but could be calculated from the Durbin-Watson statistic or directly estimated from residuals.

From the discussion in this section, it will be clear that the computer has had a tremendous impact on applied econometric work of this kind in recent years. Simultaneous equation estimation methods are easily accessible, and re-estimation as the sample period extends itself or as data revisions are published is entirely feasible. The possible size of systems of equations has rapidly increased, being highly correlated with computer technology, and it is true to say that the analyses of non-linear models described in this section have only been possible since the advent of the computer.

APPENDIX TO CHAPTER 4

The final form of dynamic econometric models

We consider the general G-equation linear model, and separate the predetermined variables into truly exogenous variables and lagged endogenous variables. (Lagged values of exogenous variables are accommodated by treating them as different exogenous variables). Assuming that the maximal lag in any endogenous variable is of r periods, we write the model in structural form as follows:

$$\mathbf{B}_0 \mathbf{y}_t + \mathbf{B}_1 \mathbf{y}_{t-1} + \ldots + \mathbf{B}_r \mathbf{y}_{t-r} + \Gamma \mathbf{x}_t = \mathbf{u}_t .$$

It is convenient in what follows to use a β-notation for coefficients of both current and lagged endogenous variables, and to reserve γ's for coefficients of truly exogenous variables. The $\mathbf{B}_l$ matrices are all $G{\times}G$, and the normalisation rule sets the diagonal elements of $\mathbf{B}_0$ equal to 1; if a specific y-variable does not appear with a given lag in any equation, then the corresponding column of $\mathbf{B}_l$ is zero. An ordinary algebraic representation is obtained by writing

$$\sum_{i=1}^{G} \sum_{l=0}^{r} \beta_{gil}\, y_{i,\, t-l} + \sum_{k=1}^{K} \gamma_{gk}\, x_{kt} = u_{gt}, \qquad g = 1, \ldots, G.$$

The reduced form in effect recombines lagged endogenous and exogenous variables, being given by

$$\mathbf{y}_t = -\mathbf{B}_0^{-1} (\mathbf{B}_1 \mathbf{y}_{t-1} + \ldots + \mathbf{B}_r \mathbf{y}_{t-r} + \Gamma \mathbf{x}_t) + \mathbf{B}_0^{-1} \mathbf{u}_t .$$

This expresses each endogenous variable as a function of predetermined variables and error terms, and the autocorrelation properties of the reduced form error terms are the same as those of the structural disturbances: if the u's are non-autocorrelated, so are the reduced form errors. The final form equations give each endogenous variable in terms of its own past and values of exogenous variables. It is convenient to introduce $\mathbf{B}(L)$, defined by

$$\mathbf{B}(L) = \mathbf{B}_0 + \mathbf{B}_1 L + \ldots + \mathbf{B}_r L^r,$$

a matrix whose elements are polynomials in the lag operator L. $\mathbf{B}(L)$ has (g,i) element $\sum_{l=0}^{r} \beta_{gil} L^l$. The model now is

$$\mathbf{B}(L)\, \mathbf{y}_t = -\Gamma \mathbf{x}_t + \mathbf{u}_t$$

The solution

$$\mathbf{y}_t = -\mathbf{B}(L)^{-1} \Gamma \mathbf{x}_t + \mathbf{B}(L)^{-1} \mathbf{u}_t$$

will in general have infinite lags in the x-variables, giving what Theil and Boot (1962) call the final form. The final equation, in the sense of Tinbergen (1939), Goldberger (1959), and ourselves is an autoregressive equation in a single endogenous variable, containing a finite number of exogenous variables, current and lagged, giving the time path of each endogenous variable in terms of the time paths of the exogenous variables. We recall that the inverse of a matrix is given by the adjoint matrix divided by the determinant (scalar), which we can write

$$\mathbf{B}(L)^{-1} = \frac{\mathbf{b}(L)}{|\mathbf{B}(L)|},$$

where $\mathbf{b}(L)$ is the adjoint matrix of $\mathbf{B}(L)$. Substituting this in the preceding equation, and multiplying through by $|\mathbf{B}(L)|$ we obtain

$$|\mathbf{B}(L)|\mathbf{y}_t = -\mathbf{b}(L)\, \Gamma \mathbf{x}_t + \mathbf{b}(L)\, \mathbf{u}_t .$$

These are the final equations for the endogenous variables, and it is immediately clear that

(i) each final equation has the same autoregressive structure, given by the polynomial $|\mathbf{B}(L)|$, which is of degree $\leq Gr$,

(ii) finite lags in exogenous variables appear, generally different between equations,

(iii) the error terms are moving averages of the structural disturbance terms, again generally different between equations.

Thus an assessment of the stability of the model requires an examination of only one final equation, since they all have the same autoregressive structure, and in particular an examination of $|\mathbf{B}(L)|$ is required. The degree of this polynomial in L will generally be considerably less than Gr, for this only obtains if all variables appear with an r-period lag, each in a different equation. If this polynomial can be factorised into a product of factors $(1 - c_i L)$, then the stability condition is that the coefficients c_i have modulus less than 1 (cf. p.74 and Glaister, 1972, Ch. 9). This is equivalent to the condition that the "characteristic equation"

$$|\mathbf{B}_0 z^r + \mathbf{B}_1 z^{r-1} + \ldots + \mathbf{B}_{r-1} z + \mathbf{B}_r| = 0$$

has roots with modulus less than 1.

Example 1

A simple example is provided by *IE*, Exercise 3.2, with an error term added to the consumption function, as in Exercise 3.5:

$$c_t = \alpha + \beta y_t + u_t$$
$$y_t = c_t + i_t$$
$$i_t = \gamma(y_t - y_{t-1}) + g_t .$$

This can be written in the present format as follows:

$$\begin{pmatrix} 1 & -\beta & 0 \\ -1 & 1 & -1 \\ 0 & -\gamma(1-L) & 1 \end{pmatrix} \begin{pmatrix} c_t \\ y_t \\ i_t \end{pmatrix} = \begin{pmatrix} \alpha & 0 \\ 0 & 0 \\ 0 & 1 \end{pmatrix} \begin{pmatrix} 1 \\ g_t \end{pmatrix} + \begin{pmatrix} u_t \\ 0 \\ 0 \end{pmatrix} ,$$

and $|\mathbf{B}(L)| = 1 - \gamma(1-L) - \beta$. The matrix $\mathbf{B}_1$ has only one non-zero element - it is not unusual for the $\mathbf{B}_l$ matrices to be rather sparse. For convenience, we combine the right hand sides of the model equations into a 3×1 vector, and having obtained the adjoint matrix, write the final equations as

$$(1-\beta-\gamma+\gamma L) \begin{pmatrix} c_t \\ y_t \\ i_t \end{pmatrix} = \begin{pmatrix} 1-\gamma(1-L) & \beta & \beta \\ 1 & 1 & 1 \\ \gamma(1-L) & \gamma(1-L) & 1-\beta \end{pmatrix} \begin{pmatrix} \alpha+u_t \\ 0 \\ g_t \end{pmatrix}.$$

In this instance, no lagged values of the exogenous variable g_t are introduced, but the first and third equations have error terms involving current and lagged values of u, which will in general be autocorrelated even if u is non-autocorrelated. The characteristic equation

$$|\mathbf{B}_0 z + \mathbf{B}_1| = 0$$

has root

$$z = \frac{-\gamma}{1-\beta-\gamma},$$

and the model is stable if this quantity is between -1 and 1. The model is a simple example of the Hicks-Samuelson multiplier-accelerator model, the version discussed by Samuelson (1939) being as follows:

$$c_t = \alpha + \beta y_{t-1} + u_{1t}$$
$$y_t = c_t + i_t + g_t$$
$$i_t = \gamma(y_{t-1} - y_{t-2}) + u_{2t}.$$

For this model we have

$$\mathbf{B}(L) = \begin{pmatrix} 1 & -\beta L & 0 \\ -1 & 1 & -1 \\ 0 & -\gamma L(1-L) & 1 \end{pmatrix},$$

$$|\mathbf{B}(L)| = 1 - (\gamma+\beta)L + \gamma L^2,$$

so the final equations are second-order autoregressions. Stability requires that the roots of

$$z^2 - (\gamma+\beta)z + \gamma = 0$$

have modulus less than 1, and since the product of the roots is γ, we see that with the usual interpretation of γ as the capital-output ratio the model is unstable.

Example 2

An empirical example of stability analysis carried out via the characteristic equation is provided by Thomas and Stoney (1970), who examine the dynamic properties of the three-equation wage-price model of Hines (1964). The endogenous variables are the rates of change of wage rates and retail prices, and the percentage of the labour force unionized. One-period lagged values of these variables appear in the model in such a way that the characteristic equation is of second degree. Using Hines' 2SLS estimated coefficients, Thomas and Stoney find that the roots of the characteristic equation are 0.797 and 7.21, the latter value suggesting that the model is dynamically unstable. However, Thomas and Stoney argue that some of Hines' rate of change variables are inappropriately defined, particularly insofar as the timing relationships between variables are concerned, and accordingly modify the method of calculating the rate of change of prices. The resulting model, with these small changes in dynamic specification, has a third-degree characteristic equation with roots -0.88, 0.76, and 0.61, and the standard errors are such that these are all significantly below unity. Thus they conclude that "while Hines' estimated three equation model is dynamically unstable, it is possible to remove this instability by appropriately redefining the price variable". The study demonstrates the value of an examination of the stability implications of an estimated dynamic system as a validation procedure for that system.

An alternative approach is to write the reduced form of G rth-order difference equations as a first order difference equation in an augmented $\mathbf{y}$-vector, as follows (cf. Glaister, 1972, Ch. 9):

$$\begin{pmatrix} y_t \\ y_{t-1} \\ y_{t-2} \\ \vdots \\ y_{t-r+1} \end{pmatrix} = \begin{pmatrix} -B_0^{-1}B_1 & -B_0^{-1}B_2 & \cdots & & -B_0^{-1}B_r \\ I & 0 & \cdots & & 0 \\ 0 & I & \cdots & & 0 \\ \vdots & \vdots & & & \vdots \\ 0 & 0 & \cdots & I & 0 \end{pmatrix} \begin{pmatrix} y_{t-1} \\ y_{t-2} \\ y_{t-3} \\ \vdots \\ y_{t-r} \end{pmatrix} + \begin{pmatrix} -B_0^{-1}\Gamma \\ 0 \\ \vdots \\ 0 \end{pmatrix} x_t + \begin{pmatrix} B_0^{-1} \\ 0 \\ \vdots \\ 0 \end{pmatrix} u_t$$

Denoting the Gr-element vector on the left hand side by y_t^*, and the $Gr\times Gr$ matrix of coefficients by A, we now have a vector first order difference equation

$$y_t^* = Ay_{t-1}^* + \Pi_2^* x_t + v_t^*.$$

Thus in practice we need only consider first order systems, as a result of this device, and the matrix A takes the place of the matrix Π_1 introduced on p.108. Again the stability condition is that the eigenvalues of A have modulus less than 1. These eigenvalues or latent roots are obtained as the solutions of the determinantal equation

$$\begin{vmatrix} -B_0^{-1}B_1-\lambda I & -B_0^{-1}B_2 & -B_0^{-1}B_3 & \cdots & -B_0^{-1}B_r \\ I & -\lambda I & 0 & \cdots & 0 \\ 0 & I & -\lambda I & \cdots & 0 \\ \vdots & \vdots & \vdots & & \vdots \\ 0 & 0 & 0 & \cdots I & -\lambda I \end{vmatrix} = 0$$

Expanding, and assuming that r is even for convenience, this becomes

$$|\lambda^r I + B_0^{-1}B_1\lambda^{r-1} I + B_0^{-1}B_2\lambda^{r-2} I + \ldots + B_0^{-1}B_{r-1}\lambda I + B_0^{-1}B_r| = 0.$$

Multiplying through by $|B_0|$ gives

$$|B_0\lambda^r + B_1\lambda^{r-1} + B_2\lambda^{r-2} + \ldots + B_{r-1}\lambda + B_r| = 0,$$

so the stability condition is exactly as derived above. In general the number of non-zero eigenvalues will be less than the maximum possible, Gr. Note that this approach requires the calculation of the reduced form, whereas in the former approach the structural parameters were used directly.

Example 1 again

The Hicks-Samuelson model has

$$\mathbf{B}_0 = \begin{pmatrix} 1 & 0 & 0 \\ -1 & 1 & -1 \\ 0 & 0 & 1 \end{pmatrix}, \quad \text{so} \quad \mathbf{B}_0^{-1} = \begin{pmatrix} 1 & 0 & 0 \\ 1 & 1 & 1 \\ 0 & 0 & 1 \end{pmatrix},$$

and with $\mathbf{y}_t^* = (c_t, y_t, i_t, c_{t-1}, y_{t-1}, i_{t-1})'$, the coefficient matrix in the augmented first order system is

$$\mathbf{A} = \begin{pmatrix} 0 & \beta & 0 & 0 & 0 & 0 \\ 0 & \beta+\gamma & 0 & 0 & -\gamma & 0 \\ 0 & \gamma & 0 & 0 & -\gamma & 0 \\ 1 & 0 & 0 & 0 & 0 & 0 \\ 0 & 1 & 0 & 0 & 0 & 0 \\ 0 & 0 & 1 & 0 & 0 & 0 \end{pmatrix}$$

$$|\mathbf{A} - \lambda\mathbf{I}| = \lambda^4\{\lambda^2 - \lambda(\beta+\gamma) + \gamma\},$$

hence the stability condition is as obtained earlier.

APPENDIX

Methods of Economic Investigation

Case Studies Reading List, Lent Term 1971

The following collected volumes are referred to in the reading list:

C. F. Christ et al., *Measurement in Economics* (Stanford)

R. A. Gordon and L. R. Klein (eds), *Readings in Business Cycles*, (A.E.A. Readings).

A. Zellner (ed), *Readings in Economic Statistics and Econometrics*, (Little, Brown).

CONSUMPTION FUNCTION: theoretical specification, empirical evidence, consistent estimation, permanent income.

1. E. Malinvaud, *Statistical Methods of Econometrics*, Ch. 4
2. J. S. Cramer, *Empirical Econometrics*, Ch. 8
3. N. Liviatan, "Tests of the Permanent-Income Hypothesis Based on a Reinterview Savings Survey," in Christ, pp. 29-66 and Zellner, pp. 253-290. (later sections).

PRODUCTION FUNCTION: specification, identification, and estimation of Cobb-Douglas and CES production and cost functions.

1. J. S. Cramer, *Empirical Econometrics*, Ch. 10
2. A. A. Walters, *An Introduction to Econometrics*, Ch. 10, or "Production and Cost Functions; An Econometric Survey," *Econometrica*, January 1963.
3. M. Nerlove, "Returns to Scale in Electricity Supply," in Christ, pp. 167-198, Zellner, pp. 409-439, and Ch. VI of his *Estimation and Identification of Cobb-Douglas Production Functions*.
4. ——— "Recent Empirical Studies of the CES and Related Production Functions" in *The Theory and Empirical Analysis of Production*, NBER Studies in Income and Wealth Vol 31, (1967). (selectively)

INVESTMENT FUNCTION: "neoclassical" theory, dynamic behaviour, hypothesis testing: the Jorgenson model and the subsequent debate.

1. D. W. Jorgenson, "Capital Theory and Investment Behavior," *Amer. Econ. Rev.*, May 1963, also in Gordon and Klein, pp. 366-378.

2. ——— "Anticipations and Investment Behavior," Ch. 2 of J. S. Duesenberry, G. Fromm, L. R. Klein, and E. Kuh (eds), *The Brookings Quarterly Econometric Model of the United States*

3. ——— "The Theory of Investment Behavior," in R. Ferber (ed), *Determinants of Investment Behavior*, (NBER, 1967), (also comments by Tobin).

Warning: the first reference is often cited, as it was the first paper on Jorgenson's investment work to appear in print. However, students often find that it is too abbreviated to serve as a useful introduction, for it is a summary prepared for the AEA meetings, and the second and third references contain a fuller discussion.

4. R. Eisner and M. I. Nadiri, "Investment Behavior and Neoclassical Theory," *Rev. Econ. Statist.*, August 1968.

5. D. W. Jorgenson and J. A. Stephenson, "Issues in the Development of the Neoclassical Theory of Investment Behavior," *Rev. Econ. Statist.*, August 1969.

6. C. W. Bischoff, "Hypothesis Testing and the Demand for Capital Goods," *Rev. Econ. Statist.*, August 1969.

7. R. Eisner and M. I. Nadiri, "Neoclassical Theory of Investment Behavior: A Comment," *Rev. Econ. Statist.*, May 1970.

MACROECONOMETRIC MODELS: rationale, dynamic properties, simulation, forecasting, policy analysis.

1. K. F. Wallis, "Some Recent Developments in Applied Econometrics," *J. Econ. Lit.*, September 1969, Part II, and references contained therein, in particular:

2. L. R. Klein, *The Keynesian Revolution* (2nd edition) Ch. 8, 9 (for general background)

3. I. Adelman and F. L. Adelman, "The Dynamic Properties of the Klein-Goldberger Model," *Econometrica*, October 1959, also in Gordon and Klein, pp. 278-306, and Zellner, pp. 630-660.

4. D. Suits, "Forecasting and Analysis with an Econometric Model," *Amer. Econ. Rev.*, March 1962, also in Gordon and Klein, pp. 597-625, and Zellner, pp. 583-611.

5. L. R. Klein, "Econometric Analysis of the Tax Cut of 1964," Ch. 13 of J. S. Duesenberry, G. Fromm, L. R. Klein and E. Kuh (eds), *The Brookings Model: Some Further Results*.

As a particular example of a macro model:

6. M. K. Evans and L. R. Klein, *The Wharton Econometric Forecasting Model*. (This model underlies some of the chapters of M. K. Evans, *Macroeconomic Activity*, which provides general background reading on macro-models and their various sectors. A version of it is used in the Klein-Evans *Econometric Gaming* computer simulation kit, adapted for use at LSE under the name SAMMUSE, which is used in short courses from time to time. Its multiplier properties are compared with those of other models by Evans in "Reconstruction and Estimation of the Balanced Budget Multiplier," *Rev. Econ. Statist.*, February 1969.)

Postscript

The recent book *Applied Econometrics* by J. L. Bridge is a useful digest of a large quantity of empirical work, including many of the references for the first three topics on the above list.

REFERENCES

Adelman, I. and Adelman, F. L. (1959). The dynamic properties of the Klein-Goldberger model. *Econometrica*, 27, 597-625. Reprinted in Gordon and Klein (1966), Hooper and Nerlove (1970), and Zellner (1968).

Allen, R. G. D. (1938). *Mathematical Analysis for Economists*. London: Macmillan.

Almon, S. (1965). The distributed lag between capital appropriations and expenditures. *Econometrica*, 33, 178-196. Reprinted in Zellner (1968).

Arrow, K. J., Chenery, H. B., Minhas, B. S. and Solow, R. M. (1961). Capital-labor substitution and economic efficiency. *Rev. Econ. Statist.*, 43, 225-250. Reprinted in Zellner (1968).

Ball, R. J. and Drake, P. S. (1964). The relationship between aggregate consumption and wealth. *Int. Econ. Rev.*, 5, 63-81.

Bischoff, C. W. (1969). Hypothesis testing and the demand for capital goods. *Rev. Econ. Statist.*, 51, 354-368.

Boatwright, B. D. and Eaton, J. R. (1972). The estimation of investment functions for manufacturing industry in the United Kingdom. *Economica*, 39, 403-418.

Bridge, J. L. (1971). *Applied Econometrics*. Amsterdam: North-Holland.

Brown, M., and de Cani, J. S. (1963). Technological change and the distribution of income. *Int. Econ. Rev.*, 4, 289-309.

Brown, T. M. (1952). Habit persistence and lags in consumer behaviour. *Econometrica*, 20, 355-371. Reprinted in Hooper and Nerlove (1970).

Christ, C. F., *et al*. (1963). *Measurement in Economics*. Stanford: University Press.

Cramer, J. S. (1969). *Empirical Econometrics*. Amsterdam: North-Holland.

Cobb, C. W. and Douglas, P. H. (1928). A theory of production. *Amer. Econ. Rev.*, 18, (*supplement*), 139-165.

Davis, T. E. (1952). The consumption function as a tool for prediction. *Rev. Econ. Statist.*, 34, 270-277.

de Leeuw, F. (1962). The demand for capital goods by manufacturers: a study of quarterly time series. *Econometrica*, 30, 407-423.

Douglas, P. H. (1948). Are there laws of production? *Amer. Econ. Rev.*, 38, 1-41.

Duesenberry, J. S. (1949). *Income, Saving, and the Theory of Consumer Behavior.* Cambridge, Mass.: Harvard University Press.

Duesenberry, J. S., Fromm, G., Klein, L. R. and Kuh, E. (eds) (1965). *The Brookings Quarterly Econometric Model of the U.S. Economy.* Chicago: Rand McNally.

——— (1969). *The Brookings Model: Some Further Results.* Chicago: Rand McNally.

Eisner, R. and Nadiri, M. I. (1968). Investment behavior and neoclassical theory. *Rev. Econ. Statist.*, 50, 369-382.

——— (1970). Neoclassical theory of investment behavior: a comment. *Rev. Econ. Statist.*, 52, 216-222.

Evans, M. K. (1967). A study of industry investment decisions. *Rev. Econ. Statist.*, 49, 151-164.

——— (1969). *Macroeconomic Activity.* New York: Harper and Row.

——— (1969a). Reconstruction and estimation of the balanced budget multiplier. *Rev. Econ. Statist.*, 51, 14-25.

Evans, M. K. and Klein, L. R. (1968). *The Wharton Econometric Forecasting Model.* Philadelphia: University of Pennsylvania Press.

Friedman, M. (1957). *A Theory of the Consumption Function.* Princeton, N.J.: University Press for National Bureau of Economic Research.

Fuchs, V. R. (1963). Capital-labor substitution: a note. *Rev. Econ. Statist.*, 45, 436-438.

Glaister, S. (1972). *Mathematical Methods for Economists.* London: Gray-Mills.

Goldberger, A. S. (1959). *Impact Multipliers and Dynamic Properties of the Klein-Goldberger Model.* Amsterdam: North-Holland.

Goldsmith, R. W. (1955). *A Study of Saving in the United States, I.* Princeton, N.J.: University Press.

Gordon, R. A. and Klein, L. R. (eds) (1966). *Readings in Business Cycles.* London: Allen and Unwin.

Gould, J. P. (1969). The use of endogenous variables in dynamic models of investment. *Quart. J. Econ.*, 83, 580-599.

Haavelmo, T. (1947). Methods of measuring the marginal propensity to consume. *J. Amer. Statist. Ass.*, 42, 105-122. Reprinted in Hood, W. C. and Koopmans, T. C. (eds) (1953), *Studies in Econometric Method*, New York: Wiley.

Harberger, A. C. (ed) (1960). *The Demand for Durable Goods.* Chicago: University Press.

Hendry, D. F. (1973). Stochastic specification in an aggregate demand model of the United Kingdom. *Econometrica*, to appear.

Hickman, B. G. (ed) (1972). *Econometric Models of Cyclical Behavior.* New York: National Bureau of Economic Research.

Hilton, K. and Heathfield, D. F. (eds) (1970). *The Econometric Study of the United Kingdom.* London: Macmillan.

Hines, A. G. (1964). Trade unions and wage inflation in the United Kingdom, 1893-1961. *Rev. Econ. Studies*, 31, 221-252.

Hogan, W. P. (1958). Technical progress and production functions. *Rev. Econ. Statist.*, 40, 407-411.

Hooper, J. W. and Nerlove, M. (eds) (1970). *Selected Readings in Econometrics from Econometrica*. London: M.I.T. Press.

Johansen, L. (1959). Substitution versus fixed production coefficients in the theory of economic growth: a synthesis. *Econometrica*, 27, 157-176.

———(1972). *Production Functions*. Amsterdam: North-Holland.

Johnson, H. G. (1971). *Macroeconomics and Monetary Theory*. London: Gray-Mills.

Jorgenson, D. W. (1963). Capital theory and investment behavior. *Amer. Econ. Rev.*, 53, 247-259. Reprinted in Gordon and Klein (1966).

——— (1965). Anticipations and investment behavior. In Duesenberry *et al.* (1965), pp. 35-92.

——— (1967). The theory of investment behavior. In *Determinants of Investment Behavior* (ed R. Ferber), pp. 129-155. New York: National Bureau of Economic Research.

Jorgenson, D. W. and Stephenson, J. A. (1967a). Investment behavior in U.S. manufacturing, 1947-1960. *Econometrica*, 35, 169-220.

——— (1967b). The time structure of investment behavior in United States manufacturing, 1947-1960. *Rev. Econ. Statist.*, 49, 16-27.

——— (1969a). Anticipations and investment behavior in U.S. manufacturing, 1947-1960. *J. Amer. Statist. Ass.*, 64, 67-89.

——— (1969b). Issues in the development of the neoclassical theory of investment behavior. *Rev. Econ. Statist.*, 51, 346-353.

Keynes, J. M. (1936). *The General Theory of Employment, Interest and Money*. London: Macmillan.

Klein, L. R. (1950). *Economic Fluctuations in the United States, 1921-1941*. Cowles Commission Monograph 11. New York: Wiley.

——— (1953). *A Textbook of Econometrics*. Evanston, Ill.: Row, Peterson.

——— (1966). *The Keynesian Revolution* (2nd ed.). London: Macmillan.

——— (1969). Econometric analysis of the tax cut of 1964. In Duesenberry *et al.* (1969), pp. 459-472.

Klein, L. R., Ball, R. J., Hazelwood, A. and Vandome, P. (1961). *An Econometric Model of the United Kingdom*. Oxford: University Press.

Klein, L. R. and Goldberger, A. S. (1955). *An Econometric Model of the United States, 1929-1952*. Amsterdam: North-Holland.

Koyck, L. M. (1954). *Distributed Lags and Investment Analysis*. Amsterdam: North-Holland.

Kuznets, S. (1942). *Uses of National Income in Peace and War*. National Bureau of Economic Research, Occasional Paper No. 6.

L'Esperance, W. L. (1964). A case study in prediction: the market for watermelons. *Econometrica*, 32, 163-173.

Liviatan, N. (1963). Tests of the permanent income hypothesis based on a reinterview savings survey. In Christ (1963), pp. 29-59. Reprinted in Zellner (1968).

Malinvaud, E. (1966). *Statistical Methods of Econometrics*. Amsterdam: North-Holland.

Mueller, M. G. (ed) (1969). *Readings in Macroeconomics*. London: Holt, Rinehart and Winston.

Nerlove, M. (1960). The market demand for durable goods: a comment. *Econometrica*, 28, 132-142.

——— (1963). Returns to scale in electricity supply. In Christ (1963), pp. 167-198. Reprinted in Zellner (1968).

——— (1965). *Estimation and Identification of Cobb-Douglas Production Functions*. Amsterdam: North-Holland

——— (1966). A tabular survey of macroeconometric models. *Int. Econ. Rev.*, 7, 127-175.

——— (1967). Recent empirical studies of the CES and related production functions. In *The Theory and Empirical Analysis of Production* (Studies in Income and Wealth Volume 31), pp. 55-122. New York: National Bureau of Economic Research.

——— (1972). Lags in economic behavior. *Econometrica*, 40, 221-251.

Renton, G. A. (ed) (1973). *Proceedings* of Conference on Modelling of the U.K. Economy, London Business School, July 1972. London: Heinemann Educational Press.

Samuelson, P. A. (1939). Interactions between the multiplier analysis and the principle of acceleration. *Rev. Econ. Statist.*, 21, 75-78. Reprinted in Mueller (1969).

Solow, R. M. (1957). Technical change and the aggregate production function. *Rev. Econ. Statist.*, 39, 312-320. Reprinted in Mueller (1969) and Zellner (1968).

Stone, R. and Rowe, D. A. (1956). Aggregate consumption and investment functions for the household sector considered in the light of British experience. *Nationalokonomisk Tidsskrift*, 94, 1-32.

——— (1960). The durability of consumer's durable goods. *Econometrica*, 28, 407-416. Reprinted in Hooper and Nerlove (1970) and Zellner (1968).

Suits, D. B. (1955). An econometric model of the watermelon market. *J. Farm. Econ.*, 37, 237-251.

——— (1962). Forecasting and analysis with an econometric model. *Amer. Econ. Rev.*, 52, 104-132. Reprinted in Gordon and Klein (1966) and Zellner (1968).

Theil, H. and Boot, J. C. G. (1962). The final form of econometric equation systems. *Rev. Int. Statist. Inst.*, 30, 136-152. Reprinted in Zellner (1968).

Thomas, R. L. and Stoney, P. J. M. (1970). A note on the dynamic properties of the Hines inflation model. *Rev. Econ. Studies*, 37, 286-294.

Tinbergen, J. (1939). *Statistical Testing of Business-Cycle Theories, II: Business Cycles in the U.S.A., 1919-1932.* Geneva: League of Nations.

——— (1951). *Business Cycles in the United Kingdom, 1870-1914.* Amsterdam: North-Holland.

Tobin, J. (1967). Comment (on Jorgenson, 1967). In *Determinants of Investment Behavior* (ed. R. Ferber), pp. 156-160. New York: National Bureau of Economic Research.

Wallis, K. F. (1969). Some recent developments in applied econometrics: dynamic models and simultaneous equation systems. *J. Econ. Lit.*, 7, 771-796.

——— (1972). *Introductory Econometrics.* London: Gray-Mills.

Walters, A. A. (1963). Production and cost functions: an econometric survey. *Econometrica*, 31, 1-66.

——— (1968). *An Introduction to Econometrics.* London: Macmillan.

Wold, H. O. A. (1958). A case study of interdependent versus causal chain systems. *Rev. Int. Statist. Inst.*, 26, 5-25.

Zellner, A. (ed) (1968). *Readings in Economic Statistics and Econometrics.* Boston: Little, Brown.

Zellner, A., Huang, D. S. and Chau, L. C. (1965). Further analysis of the short-run consumption function with emphasis on the role of liquid assets. *Econometrica*, 33, 571-581.

AUTHOR INDEX